SIGNING Naturally

VISTA

AMERICAN SIGN LANGUAGE SERIES
FUNCTIONAL NOTIONAL APPROACH

SIGNING
Naturally

TEACHER'S
CURRICULUM
GUIDE

L E V E L
2

ELLA MAE LENTZ / KEN MIKOS / CHERI SMITH
EDITED BY LISA CAHN

DawnSignPress

Berkeley, CA

Production directed by *Joe Dannis*

Illustrations by *Patricia Pearson, Brian Clarke*

Sign Illustrations by *Paul Setzer*

Sign Models by *Tina Jo Breindel, Sue Burnes*

Published by DawnSignPress

Printed in the United States of America

ISBN: 0-915035-08-1

10 9 8 7 6 5 4 3 2

Attention schools, distributors and teachers: Quantity discounts and special purchase arrangements for teachers and schools are available.
For information, contact:

9080-A Activity Road, San Diego, CA 92126
619/549-5330 Voice   619/549-5333 TDD   619/549-2200 FAX

TABLE OF CONTENTS

Language Functions	Grammar
give reason	topic-comment structure
make request	weak hand as reference
ask where	locative classifiers
give specific location	yes/no questions
correct and confirm information	wh-questions
open conversations	ordinal numbers
	numbers: 101 – 109,
	multiples of 100 to 1,000

complain about others	recurring time signs:
make suggestion	EVERY-(time sign)
make request	continuous time signs:
ask for permission	ALL-(time sign)
express concern	temporal aspect:
decline, explain why	recurring, continuous
agree, with condition	inflecting verbs
agree, tell shortcomings	role shifting
ask for clarification	conditional sentences
	clock numbers

ask/tell when	when clauses
tell about life events	phrasing for sequencing events
ask nationality of name	contrastive structure
narrate family immigration	possessive forms: POSS, 'S
history	descriptive and locative
correct and elaborate	classifiers (Breakaway)
	numbers: 110 – 119, dates
	and addresses

PREFACE

Signing Naturally – Level 2 is part of the *Signing Naturally* series developed by the instructional staff at Vista Community College in Berkeley, California. Included in this series are four levels of language instruction with detailed lesson plans for instructors of American Sign Language. Each level is approximately 100–120 hours of classroom instruction with accompanying *Teacher's Cumulative Review* videotape.

In addition to the above materials, an orientation videotape for teachers is included in the Program Series package.

Teachers using this Curriculum Guide should send the attached card to receive a desk copy of *Signing Naturally: Student Videotexts and Workbook* – Level 2 to supplement classroom instruction.

ACKNOWLEDGEMENTS

Since Fall 1984, the FIPSE-project staff with the support of the following people, educational institutions and agencies, have been able to develop the first ASL curriculum. There are several people we would particularly like to thank:

Maureen Knightly, Vista Assistant Dean, for her assistance in writing the original grant proposal that made this curriculum possible.

Lisa Cahn, project editor, for her tireless dedication to thoroughness and accuracy, for typing and editing the many revisions, for her various home remedies, and for livening up the long hours with donkey stories.

Dennis Cokely, Carol Padden, and Ted Supalla, our consultants, for their insights and useful suggestions, and particularly to consultant Peter Shaw, who remained available long after the job was done.

Ben Bahan, Marlon Kuntze, and Jamie Tucker, language analysts, for their willingness to share their linguistic knowledge and insights and to serve as language models, and for entertaining us with their humor and wit.

Mary Hill Telford, resident transcriber/language model, for her unabashed enthusiasm, for taking pride in our work, for lending the kind of understanding that comes from a good friend, and for sharing freely her colorful use of ASL.

The many members of the Deaf community who were willing to participate in our language study. Also the Deaf actors who made possible the filming of the curriculum language videotapes.

Scott Luebking for his invaluable programming assistance which allowed us to use the UNIX computer system to analyze language samples.

The test-site programs: California State University (Northridge and Hayward), Columbus Technical Institute, Gallaudet University, Iowa Western Community College, Madonna College, Mt. San Antonio Community College, Northeastern University, Ohlone College, San Diego Community College, and Vista Community College.

All the test-site teachers for helping to evaluate the curriculum. We would especially like to thank Dennis Berrigan for his dedication, encouragement and commitment to providing us with the most comprehensive evaluation possible.

Administration and staff of Vista Community College for their cooperation and generous in-kind contribution.

The Fund for the Improvement of Postsecondary Education for the three-year funding that enabled this project to be drafted and tested, and to Diana Hayman, our FIPSE Program Officer, for her on-going support of innovations in ASL teaching.

We would especially like to thank our families and special friends, jokingly referred to as the "ASL widows," for their support and patience over the past years.

INTRODUCTION

Signing Naturally is a curriculum guide for teachers of American Sign Language (ASL). We wrote it to help teachers plan a sequence of lessons for four levels of language learning. Each of the four levels equals approximately 100 – 120 hours of instruction. This level has ten instructional units complete with lesson plans, activities, and materials. In addition, this level has two Cumulative Review units which are based on videotape presentations designed to introduce cultural behaviors, values and norms.

Signing Naturally takes students who have no knowledge of Sign Language to the point where they can function comfortably in a wide variety of situations in the Deaf community. Since students will most likely continue their learning in the Deaf community, it is essential that they learn appropriate behaviors, showing awareness of and respect for Deaf culture. Deaf culture is taught throughout the curriculum. Through videotape presentations, native signers model appropriate language and cultural behaviors in various situations. Discussions, activities and readings also reinforce what students learn from the videotapes.

Functional-Notional Approach

Before designing the curriculum, we studied different approaches to second-language teaching. We needed an approach that emphasized interpersonal communication to help students achieve communicative competence. We selected the functional-notional approach, which focuses on the "functions" or communicative purposes of people's everyday interaction. For example, do they want to introduce themselves? Do they want to invite someone to their home? Do they want to direct someone to do something? Do they want to talk about a movie, book or event? Do they want to tell a story?

We emphasize functions that help students establish and maintain social relationships. We introduce polite, informal register of ASL in the first two levels. We begin with personal information and move to impersonal; we move from naming things that are present to talking about things not present; we begin by talking about concrete things and progress to talking about abstract ideas. Grammatical structures introduced are determined by the function in the unit; that is, students learn grammar in the context of communicative activities. Activities are varied to allow students to use different learning strategies to practice what they have learned. Role-play situations which predict everyday deaf-hearing encounters are used to contextualize and give meaning to the function. The indirect benefit of these situations for students is the development of cultural awareness and cross-cultural adjustment skills.

Teaching Philosophy

We designed the units with the following principles in mind:

1) Students learn language best when lessons are presented in context.
2) Students retain language best when activities are meaningful and experiential.
3) Students develop comprehension skills more quickly than their expressive skills.

Therefore, all lessons are designed to be presented in ASL, avoiding the use of voice, written English or glosses, and teachers are encouraged to always sign slightly beyond the students' expressive ability.

Organization of Level 2

Level 2 contains Units 13-17 and a Cumulative Review unit. Each unit in Level 2 builds upon the topics, vocabulary and grammar introduced in previous lessons in Level 1.

Whereas Level 1 introduced language concepts related to people, places and things within the immediate environment, Level 2 encourages students to talk about people in a more abstract way and to talk about the environment removed from the classroom, i.e., at home or other parts of the country. Students also learn to narrate events that occurred in the past, as opposed to telling what is happening currently.

Level 2, students learn to locate things around the house, ask for solutions to everyday problems, tell about life events, describe objects, and talk about weekend activities. In the Cumulative Review for those units, students learn appropriate cultural behaviors for directing and maintaining attention, and a way of talk that keeps others informed. They also learn strategies such as controlling the pace of conversation and resuming conversations after an interruption.

Organization of Instructional Units

The **Overview** at the beginning of each unit shows the teacher, at a glance, what is covered in the unit. A dialogue format shows the basic functions taught, followed by a sample dialogue, a list of vocabulary introduced, the sentence structures, grammar, and conversation strategies covered, sign illustrations that appear in the unit, and finally, a list of the Materials needed for the unit.

Each unit is then divided into five major sections:

Introduction shows teachers how to introduce grammar and vocabulary in context. Teachers are provided with step-by-step teaching strategies and materials to help them present the lesson in ASL.

Sign Production shows teachers how to drill students to develop the signing skills that lead to fluency. Sign Production activities are usually focused on smaller units of language — vocabulary and sentence structures rather than dialogues or narrative practice.

Extended Comprehension shows teachers how to reinforce and expand on the functions, grammar and vocabulary presented in the lesson. This section is for comprehension building. Teacher's narratives should be a regular part of the class: telling anecdotes, stories about what happened to you, reminiscing about events in class. Students develop strategies for figuring out meaning without understanding every sign.

Narrative Practice provides teachers with activities that help develop techniques for narrating. Students develop skills for role shifting, spatial structuring, sequencing events, and establishing time references.

Interaction provides teachers with communicative activities that range from structured to spontaneous, allowing students to integrate what they've learned on a discourse level. Students learn appropriate listener responses, and rehearse conversation strategies.

Breakaways provide teachers with a way to vary activities, develop rapport in class, and work on other aspects of ASL. Breakaways are divided into five kinds of activities: fingerspelling, numbers, language building, classifiers and team building. These activities can be done at any time within the unit, and repeated as necessary.

> **Fingerspelling and Numbers** activities provide students with practice in mastering these features of the language.

> **Language-building** activities give students an opportunity to review and apply what they've learned in a variety of exercises designed to stimulate interaction.

> **Classifier** activities help students develop skills to describe and locate things using appropriate classifier signs. These activities also help students to visualize objects and their surroundings, enabling them to clearly structure objects within the signing space.

> **Team-building** activities build rapport and lower anxiety in the classroom.

Organization of Cumulative Review Units

These units are based on videotape presentations. The language presented on tape is designed to recycle language functions students have learned. The videotapes present cultural behaviors and topics relevant to cross-cultural interactions. Conversation strategies are rehearsed. Students also see live storytelling, and develop role-shifting skills for telling narratives.

Student Videotext and Workbook

Each student should have a copy of the *Student Videotexts and Workbook* for Level 2. These materials provide students with a way to review, practice and retain what they have learned in class.

Our experience with Sign Language books led us to conclude that videotape is the most effective medium for Sign Language materials. We found that students use books as a reference for remembering signs, but unfortunately, most Sign Language books associate English with signs. This defeats the purpose of the curriculum, which encourages students to think only in signs.

The key to ASL is movement. On videotape we can show correct sign forms, how a sign is used in a sentence, how a sign form is influenced by the sign that precedes or follows. We can show where facial expressions occur in the sentence, how body, head, and eye movements are used for phrasing. We can handle more complicated ASL features such as spatial referencing, classifiers, verb inflections, and role shifting, all of which gather meaning from movement. The *Videotexts and Workbook* also include a variety of activities which allow students to check their comprehension and practice signs. Most are designed as enrichment activities to be assigned as homework, although some activities can be used in the classroom. Short, sometimes humorous, sometimes artistic, sometimes treasured folklore stories make *Videotexts* the invaluable reference for students throughout their language learning.

Teacher Preparation

We suggest the following:

1) View the *Teacher's Orientation Videotape* which is designed to demonstrate various activity types and discuss language principles central to the curriculum (optional).

2) Read the entire curriculum to familiarize yourself with how functions, topics and grammar features are sequenced and recycled throughout the level. Look particularly at the Overviews to get a general idea of what the student will learn in each unit.

3) Familiarize yourself with the Transcription Conventions (following this Introduction) to help you understand the glosses and symbols used in the units. Long passages of sign glosses in the text should be memorized or prepared in advance so that you do not have to read and sign simultaneously in class.

4) Read the unit thoroughly to get familiar with the activities. Check the materials in the Materials Appendix and know where they fit into the lesson; note which materials need to be photocopied or made into transparencies, and which you need to develop or bring to class yourself.

5) Review the whole unit and make an outline for the classroom. You should avoid reading the unit as you teach, and only refer to the book to refresh your memory or to use specific sentences for drill.

6) To add variety to the class, you may want to teach from two units at a time, particularly for three-hour classes. You should feel free to add favorite activities of your own to enrich the lesson.

7) At the end of each unit, assign homework in the *Student Videotext and Workbook*. You should familiarize yourself with the material in the *Workbook* and have some class time set aside to discuss the assignments. You may want to assign some of the activities during the unit rather than all of them at the end.

Strategies for Introducing Signs

1) Avoid giving or accepting English equivalents:

   a) avoid mouthing full words
   b) avoid using voice
   c) avoid fingerspelling (except for proper names or words commonly fingerspelled in ASL)
   d) ignore students' fingerspelling (don't encourage it)

2) Suggestions on how to introduce or explain signs for:

   ### concrete concepts

   a) point to or show the things themselves
   b) draw pictures of things if they are not present
   c) act out or describe things using classifiers or gestures

   ### abstract concepts

   a) act out emotions or situations (use stereotypes if helpful and not offensive), i.e., erase your forehead to describe the sign FORGET
   b) tell students that the new sign is the opposite of another sign they know, i.e., if students know FORGET, teach REMEMBER as the opposite
   c) use other signs with similar meanings (synonyms), i.e., for DISGUSTED, use LITTLE-BIT MAD, THINK IX PEA-BRAINED, NOT+LIKE, etc.
   d) give several signs in the same category, or associate the sign with equivalents, i.e., to teach HISTORY, sign ENGLISH, MATH, SCIENCE, etc.

3) After introducing a sign, use the sign in different contexts to make sure students understand its meaning.

We hope, with this *Signing Naturally* series, future ASL students will sign naturally, interact comfortably and show awareness of and respect for the Deaf community. We hope this curriculum guide contributes to preserving the integrity of the language, and encourages more Deaf instructors to enter the field. This curriculum, along with on-going ASL linguistic research and original literary works being produced by the Deaf community, will continue to demonstrate that American Sign Language is the subtle, elegant, powerful language of a rich, complex culture.

Transcription Conventions:
Symbols Used to Write ASL

Symbol	Example	Explanation
WORD	SIGN DEAF	An English word in capital letters stands for an ASL sign (this word is called a **gloss**). The meaning of the sign and the English word may not be exactly the same.
fs-	fs-BOB fs-FEB	"fs-" is the abbreviation for a **finger-spelled word**.
#	#CAR #EARLY	A pound sign (#) indicates a **fingerspelled loan sign**.
- -	OH-I-SEE THANK-YOU	When the words for sign glosses are separated by a hyphen, they represent a **single sign**.
+	NOT+HERE MOTHER+FATHER TRUE+WORK	A plus sign between the words for sign glosses is used for both **compound signs** and **contractions**.
/	REAL/TRUE BOLD/TOUGH	A slash between words for sign glosses is used when **one sign** has two **different** English **equivalents**.
" "	"wave-no" "what" "wave-left"	Quotation marks around lower-case words indicate a **gesture-like sign**.
! !	!BORED! !MUST!	Exclamation marks are used for **emphatic form;** the sign is stressed or emphasized.
++	DIFFERENT++ WORK++	Plus signs after a word indicate **repetitions** of the sign. The symbol is also used for habitual or frequentative inflection.
-cont	USE-*cont*	The suffix "-*cont*" indicates **continuous** inflection on verbs.
-char	MAD-*char*	The suffix "-*char*" indicates the modulation on a sign showing a **"characteristic"** behavior or trait.
[ ]	[NEAR]	Brackets show that a sign is **optional**, not required in a sentence.
(2h)	(2h)#DO++	(2h) stands for **"two-handed"** and is used when a sign commonly one-handed is made with both hands.
(2h)alt.	(2h)alt.GUESS	The symbol "alt." indicates that both hands move in an **alternating** manner.

Symbol	Example	Explanation
wg	ECL:5wg	The suffix "wg" shows that the fingers wiggle when making the sign.
( )	(nod) (shake head) (draws shape)	Words in parentheses indicate an **action or movement** made without a sign, sometimes with linguistic meaning (i.e., negative or affirmative responses).
	(city)	Parentheses are also used for **variable signs** that change in different contexts.
(wh)	(wh)3	The symbol "wh" stands for weak hand and is used when the sign is made with the **non-dominant hand.**
[(wh)B*"shelf"*/IX-loc...**]**		Brackets are used around **separate signs made at the same time;** the "wh" symbol indicates which sign is made with the non-dominant hand.
BRING*"here"* MOTHER*"left"* TAKE-FROM*"table"*		**Spatial or locative information** about a sign is italicized and in quotes, immediately after the sign gloss.
you-SHOW-TO-*her* *he*-GIVE-TO-*me*		Italicized words before and after inflecting verbs indicate the **subject and object** of the verb.

Clarification of Some Puzzling Glosses

IX   Short for INDEX, IX indicates **pointing** and is used for third person pronouns (he, she, it, him, her). Specific referents are indicated by italicized words in quotation marks, immediately following the gloss (i.e., IX*"father"*).

IX-loc   IX-loc means "there" and is used to indicate the **location** of an object or place. Specific information is given in italics and quotation marks immediately after the sign gloss (i.e., IX-loc*"under table"*).

IX-dir   IX-dir is used when the pointing gives **directions** or traces a route to a place (i.e., IX-dir*"around the corner to the right"*).

IX-*thumb* **IX-*index*** **IX-*middle*** **IX-*ring*** **IX-*pinkie*** **IX-*mult***   These signs are all used in the process of listing people or things on the non-dominant hand. Listing usually begins with the thumb. IX-*mult* (see sign illustration on p. 156) is used when presenting all items on the list.

POSS   POSS is used for the **possessive pronoun.** Specific referents are given in italics and quotation marks when necessary (i.e., POSS*"father"* to mean "father's").

Symbols for Non-Manual Behaviors

Symbol	Example	Explanation
__q	<u>YOU EAT FINISH.</u> ^q	yes/no question
__whq	<u>YOU NAME "what".</u> ^{whq}	wh-word question
__neg	<u>EAT NOT-YET.</u> ^{neg}	negation
__t	<u>YESTERDAY ME SICK.</u> ^t	topic (includes relative clause)
__when	<u>...LUNCH FINISH,...</u> ^{when}	similar to conditional sentence, indicating when something happens
__cond	<u>fs-IF WE STAND...</u> ^{cond}	conditional clause — always the first part of a sentence
__neg/q	<u>NOT HURT.</u> ^{neg/q}	negative and yes/no question markers at the same time
__t/q	<u>SEE WOMAN IX-loc...</u> ^{t/q}	topic and yes/no question markers at the same time
__nod	<u>ME FINISH SEND-*you*.</u> ^{nod}	assertion
__rhet	<u>HOW ME COME-TO, HOW++.</u> ^{rhet}	rhetorical question
< *rs:* >	< *rs:woman* "hmm" FIRST-*thumb*++...>.	role shifting: the word following "*rs:*" indicates the person whose "role" the signer is assuming; the signer maintains the role until the closing bracket (>)
,	<u>PAPER IX-loc, PICK-UP.</u> ^t	short pause in sentence
.	WORK FINISH.	end of sentence

Adverbial Non-Manual Behaviors

Symbol	Example	Explanation

Relative distance/time

<u>cs</u>	<u>cs</u> YESTERDAY IX...	close by in time or location ("cs" stands for cheek to shoulder)
<u>far away</u>	<u>far away</u> IX-dir *"all the way"*	marker for "off in the distance"

Size and shape

<u>mm</u>	<u>mm</u> MEDIUM	normal or with regularity
<u>oo</u>	<u>oo</u> THIN	abnormally small or thin
<u>cha</u>	<u>cha</u> MAN DCL*"extremely tall"*	abnormally large or tall
puff [cheeks]	<u>　　</u> DCL:claw *"swollen* puff cheeks *foot"*-hold	rounded, swollen or puffy (also used for great quantity)
tight lips	<u>tight lips</u> DCL*"steel ball"*	very solid, dense, hard

Manner

stress	<u>stress</u> IX BUSY++	marker for intensity
<u>th</u>	<u>th</u> MESS-UP	careless or damaged

Responses

<u>grimace</u>	<u>grimace</u> REAL/TRUE++ "wow"	these markers all show different affects or feelings when interacting with others
concern	<u>concern</u> REAL/TRUE++	
<u>smug</u>	<u>smug</u> CRITICIZE/CORRECT	
<u>mad</u>	<u>mad</u> BAWL-OUT++	

Symbols for Classifiers

Symbol	Explanation

Symbol

Explanation

DCL"_____"

Descriptive classifier sign used to describe an object or a person. What is described is italicized and in quotation marks (i.e., DCL*"curly hair"*). Sometimes referred to as size and shape specifiers or SASSes.

LCL:__"_____"

Locative classifier sign representing an object in a specific place (and sometimes indicating movement). Handshape is given, followed by spatial or locative information italicized and in quotation marks (i.e., LCL:B*"leaf drifting to the ground"*).

SCL:__"_____"

Semantic classifier sign representing a category of nouns such as vehicle or person. Handshape is given, followed by information about specific movement italicized and in quotation marks (i.e., SCL:1*"person walking stiffly and hurriedly"*).

BCL"_____"

Body classifier sign in which the body "enacts" the verb of the sentence. Role shifting is usually required. Specific action is described in italics and quotation marks (i.e., BCL*"acting macho"*, BCL*"put arms around friend"*).

ICL"_____"

Instrument classifier sign in which part of the body (usually the hands) manipulates an object (i.e., ICL*"turn crank"* or ICL*"play jacks"*).

BPCL:__"_____"

Bodypart classifier sign representing a specific part of the body doing the action. Handshape is often indicated and specific action is described in italics and quotation marks (i.e., (2h)BPCL:1*"crossing legs"*, (2h)BPCL:B*"taps foot"*).

PCL:__"_____"

Plural classifier sign, indicating either specific number or non-specific number (i.e., PCL:3*"people walking"*, PCL:4*"long line of people"*, PCL:5*"hordes of"*).

ECL:__"_____"

Element classifier sign representing an element of the earth, such as rain, wind/smoke/gas, fire and light. These are usually made with either the 5-handshape or the 1-handshape, i.e., ECL:5wg*"waterfall"*, ECL:1*"water dripping from a faucet"*.

SIGNING

Naturally

UNIT 13

LOCATING THINGS AROUND THE HOUSE
O V E R V I E W

DIALOGUE FORMAT:

Signer A: give reason, make request
B: agree, ask where
A: give specific location
B: ask for confirmation
A: confirm or correct

SAMPLE DIALOGUE:

Signer A: ME LEAVE COMB IX-loc LIBRARY,
$$\overline{\text{NOT-MIND FOR+ME GET.}}^{\ q}$$

B: $\overline{\text{#OK, WHERE.}}^{\ whq}$

A: $\overline{\text{KNOW LIBRARY, ENTER, SHELF+.}}^{\ t/q \quad \ t}$
"wave-left" "wave-up" COMB IX-loc.

B: $\overline{\text{SHELF+ "wave-left" "wave-up" COMB IX-loc.}}^{\ q}$

$\overline{}^{\ nod}$
A: THAT-ONE.

VOCABULARY:

house related	quantifiers	numbers	other
rooms in a house	#ALL	101 – 109	GONE
parts of a house	ALL	multiples of 100 to 1,000	LOOK-AT
building materials	MOST		DISGUSTED
other descriptions of a house	MANY		BE-LOST
furniture	SEVERAL		LOOK-FOR
accessories/fixtures	SOME		FIND
big appliances	NONE		

objects	objects	objects
DICTIONARY	fs-GLUE	MATCH
RUBBER+ERASE	NEWSPAPER	SAFETY-PIN
TAPE	MAGAZINE	UMBRELLA
SCISSORS	BROOM	HEADACHE+MEDICINE (or) fs-ASPIRIN
SIGN+LANGUAGE VIDEOTAPE	fs-NAIL	fs-BILLS
PLANT	DCL"envelope"	TIME+DCL"shape of clock"
PICTURE+DCL"shape of frame"	#TV+fs-GUIDE	SLEEP+fs-BAG
FILE+FOLD++	SCREWDRIVER	CAMERA
SHOE ICL"polish"	NAIL-CLIPPERS	CALENDAR
PENNY++	NEEDLE+STRING (thread)	
STAMP	CANDLE	

SENTENCE STRUCTURES:

tell location of room

(establish reference point)	(tell new location in relation to reference point)	(identify room)

describe location of furniture

$\overline{\text{ENTER,}}^{\ t}$	(room)	(furniture)	(classifier indicating location)

identify a specific location in another room

			t			
KNOW	(name of room)	ENTER	IX-loc *"part of room"*	SHELF CABINET DRAWER	FIRST SECOND THIRD TOP BOTTOM MIDDLE "wave-left" "wave-right" CORNER	[(wh)LCL:B*"surface"*/ IX-loc*"location of object in relation to surface"*]

GRAMMAR:

topic-comment structure
ordinal numbers: FIRST, SECOND, THIRD
reference points marking locations of non-present objects
locative classifiers
semantic classifiers (SCL:1, SCL:bent-V)

CONVERSATION STRATEGIES:

opening conversations with yes/no questions
confirming and correcting information

SIGN ILLUSTRATIONS:

IX-dir*"to right"* (see p. 9)
LCL:B(palm out) (see p. 12)
LCL:B(palm down) (see p. 12)
LCL:C(palm out) (see p. 12)
DCL:C(palm down, sweeps) (see p. 12)
SCL:bent-V (see p. 12)
[(wh)LCL:B*"surface"*/IX-loc] (see p. 14)
"wave-no" (see p. 17)

MATERIALS:

"The House," "Floor Plan," "Living Room," "Bedroom," "Kitchen," and "Bathroom" transparencies
Survey Forms
"The Office" transparency
"Where's the TV Guide?" transparency
"Design Your Living Room" worksheets
"Lost Shoe" picture sequence
"Then What Happened?" picture sequences (Breakaway)

floor plan of your own home
toy furniture
magazine pictures

INTRODUCTION

Around the House

1. Show "The House" and "Floor Plan" transparencies (see Materials Appendix, pp. 23 – 24). Introduce the following vocabulary:

frontal view	rooms	describe home
FRONT+ENTER	LIVING-ROOM	(#) FLOOR
GARAGE	BED+ROOM	OLD
fs-YARD	EAT+ROOM	NEW
fs-ROOF	KITCHEN	DCL*"trim"*
fs-PORCH	FAMILY+ROOM	DCL*"steps"*
SWIMMING+fs-POOL	CLOSET	
FENCE	BATHROOM	materials
STAIRS	WASH-CLOTHES (laundry)	WOOD
fs-ATTIC		STUCCO/CEMENT
BASEMENT		RED+DCL*"brick"*
fs-AC (air conditioning)		GLASS (windows)
		STONE+DCL:claw *"stone wall"*

Then ask students about their homes, i.e.:

• what kind of building (house, apartment, condominium)

• what it looks like (number of floors, color, materials, trim)

• how many rooms (and what they are)

For example:

                    _____whq
T: YOU LIVE WHERE.

                     _____q
YOU LIVE HOUSE.

                                  q
YOUR HOUSE 2 FLOOR+.

             t   whq
YOUR HOUSE, COLOR "what".

             t   whq
YOUR HOUSE, WOOD, STUCCO/CEMENT, RED+DCL*"brick"* WHICH.

             t   whq
YOUR HOUSE, HOW-MANY BED+ROOM.

2. Show the "Living Room" and "Bedroom" transparencies (see Materials Appendix, pp. 25 – 26). Introduce the following vocabulary:

living room	bedroom	accessories/fixtures
FURNITURE	BED	PICTURE+PAINTING
COFFEE TABLE	DRAWER (dresser)	CURTAINS
FIREPLACE	MIRROR	BLINDS
CHAIR+DCL:C"couch"	CLOSET	LIGHT+ECL"light on" (lamp)
SHELF	BED+DCL"cover"	PLANT+DCL"shape of plant"
fs-RUG	BLANKET	FOLD+CHAIR
ROCKING-CHAIR	PILLOW (or BED+SOFT)	
#TV	fs-DESK (or TABLE)	
fs-STEREO	TELEPHONE	
	TIME+DCL"shape of clock"	

Review vocabulary by asking students general questions about their own living rooms and bedrooms, including:

- what size (big, small)

- what color

- what furniture

- other fixtures in the room

For example:

> | $\overline{\text{\hspace{3em}t\hspace{3em}}}$ | $\overline{\text{whq}}$ |
> |---|---|
>
> **T:** YOUR #TV, DCL"portable", DCL"console" WHICH.
>
> $\overline{\text{\hspace{10em}}}$ $\overline{\text{t}}$ $\overline{\text{whq}}$
> YOUR CHAIR+DCL:C"couch", COLOR "what".
>
> $\overline{\text{\hspace{14em}q}}$
> YOU HAVE ROCKING-CHAIR, YOU.
>
> $\overline{\text{\hspace{18em}q}}$
> YOUR LIVING-ROOM HAVE LIGHT+ECL"light on"(lamp).
>
> $\overline{\text{\hspace{12em}whq}}$
> DCL"table lamp", DCL"floor lamp" WHICH.

3. Show the "Kitchen" and "Bathroom" transparencies (see Materials Appendix, pp. 27 – 28). Introduce the following vocabulary:

kitchen		bathroom
fs-STOVE	FREEZER	[fs-SINK]
fs-REF	MICROWAVE or fs-MWO	TOILET+CHAIR
fs-SINK	DISHWASHER or fs-DW	MIRROR
OVEN or fs-OVEN	DCL"countertop"	BATH (tub)
(ELECTRIC, #GAS)	TIME+DCL"clock"	SHOWER
CABINET	CEILING-FAN	TOWEL
		SOAP
		TOILET PAPER
		HAVE-COLD PAPER (tissue)

Review vocabulary by asking students questions about their own kitchens and bathrooms, including:

- is the room color coordinated (appliances, sink, walls, floor, cabinets)
- what color was the room before, and what color now
- is the stove/heater electric or gas

For example:

_____t   whq _____q
T: YOUR fs-STOVE, fs-REF, COLOR "what", SAME-AS *"each other"*.
_____t   whq _____whq
YOUR BATHROOM, DCL *"wall"* COLOR "what". BEFORE COLOR "what".
_____t   whq
YOUR fs-STOVE, ELECTRIC, #GAS WHICH.

SIGN PRODUCTION

"Asking Questions About the House"

Purpose: To review question forms and practice new vocabulary.

1. Write on the board:

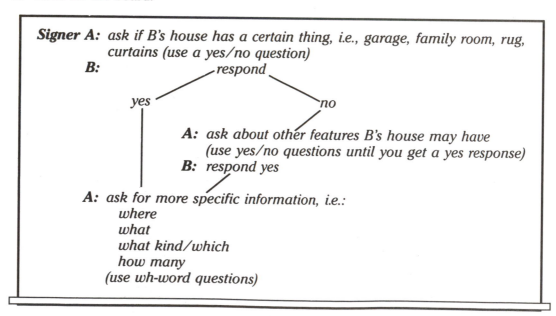

Tell the class that one effective way to **open conversations** is with yes/no questions. When the other person responds affirmatively, it is easy to ask more information with wh-word questions.

2. Review vocabulary by pointing to different items on the transparencies and calling on students to role play Signer A. They should follow the dialogue format, asking you questions about the item you pointed out.

Sample dialogue:

     T: (point to garage)

                                  _____q

     A: YOU HAVE GARAGE, YOU.

T (as B): YES.

                                                              q

     A: SEPARATE, [#OR] [(wh)LCL:C*"house"*/LCL:C*"room attached to house"*,

          whq

     WHICH.

T (as B): (respond with information)

---

3. Divide the class into pairs to practice the dialogue. Point to different items on the transparencies and have Signer A ask questions about those items. Then have them switch roles and continue with other items on the transparencies.

INTERACTION

Group Survey: What's in Your House?

Purpose: To rehearse the vocabulary and question forms in a group situation.

1. Divide the class into groups of four. Pass out a different Survey Form (see Materials Appendix, pp. 29–32) to each group member. Student 1 begins by asking the group all the questions on his/her survey form. After s/he has filled out the form, Student 2 begins. Continue until Students 3 and 4 have completed their forms.

   Variation: This activity may take one to two hours to complete. As an alternative, hand out only one Survey Form at four different class sessions. This will also help to review vocabulary.

2. Ask the class about the results of their survey. For example:

   - How many students live in an apartment?
   - How many have a fireplace?
   - How many have a window above the kitchen sink?

   Record the information on the board.

Then draw a continuum on the board, and
teach the following quantifier vocabulary
as points on the continuum:

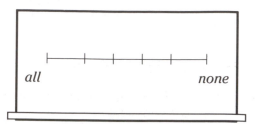

#ALL	ALL	MOST	MANY
SOME	SEVERAL*	NONE	

Based on the survey information on the board, use the quantifier vocabulary in
sentences like the following:

MOST LEARN+ER LIVE HOUSE.
MANY HAVE GARAGE.
SEVERAL HAVE FIREPLACE.
ALL LIVING-ROOM HAVE fs-RUG.
NONE BED+ROOM BLACK PAINT.
SOME BED+ROOM 1 WINDOW.
SEVERAL HAVE fs-OVEN, fs-DW, #REF COLOR SAME-AS*"all"*.
#ALL HAVE ELECTRIC fs-OVEN.

3. Have students practice quantifier vocabulary by coming up and telling about the
rest of the survey information on the board.

B R E A K A W A Y

NUMBERS

Introduce numbers 101 – 109

Sign in the following order, increasing fluency by reducing the C to bent
finger only:

101: 1+C+0+1
102: 1+C+0+2
etc.

Introduce multiples of 100 up to 1,000

Number signs 200, 300, 400 and 500 can take either the 2+C form, or
the form in which the fingers bend or wiggle in a C-shape. 600 and
above are made with 6+open-C, 7+open-C, etc.

---

*NOTE: The sign SEVERAL with "oo" non-manual behavior means "very few," and with "mm" non-manual
behavior means "several" or "quite a few." Be sure your non-manual behaviors fit the information on the board.

INTRODUCTION

Describing Where Rooms are Located

1. Show the "Floor Plan" transparency again (see Materials Appendix, p. 24). Review vocabulary and sentence structures introduced in Level 1, Unit 7, "Giving Directions on the Same Floor" (p. 125). Ask questions such as:

                         t   whq
HOUSE FRONT ENTER "area"*to-left* "what". (answer: living room)

               t   whq
LIVING-ROOM ACROSS-FROM*"left to right"* "what". (answer: dining room)

                    t   whq
EAT+ROOM IX-loc*"right"* NEXT-TO*"up, on the left"* "what". (answer: kitchen)

             t   whq
KITCHEN, ACROSS-FROM*"right to left"* "what". (answer: bedroom)

                   t   whq
BED+ROOM (wh)IX-loc, NEXT-TO*"up, on the right"* "what". (answer: other bedroom)

                       q
BATHROOM NEAR WASH-CLOTHES(laundry). (answer: no)

2. Show how to describe the floor plan of the house, beginning at the front door. Emphasize IX-dir* and "area" in your description, i.e.:

---

                       t
T: HOUSE, ENTER "area"*to-left* LIVING-ROOM.

               t
IX-dir*"to right"*, EAT+ROOM "area".

             t
IX-dir*"to left"* KITCHEN "area".

    t   mm
HALL, IX-dir*"down hall to right"* BATHROOM.

         t/mm
IX-dir*"to left"* BED+ROOM, SMALL.

                  t/far away
IX-dir*"further down on left"* BED+ROOM, LARGE, HAVE BATHROOM.

                 t/far away
IX-dir*"down to end of hallway"* EXIT, fs-DECK DCL:C*"deck"*.

                     t
KITCHEN IX-loc*"right"*, IX-dir*"continuing forward"* FAMILY+ROOM "area".

                  t
IX-loc*"right"*, GARAGE WITH WASH-CLOTHES(laundry) IX-loc.

IX-dir*"to right"*

---

*NOTE: See Transcription Conventions, p. xi, for explanation of IX-loc and IX-dir.

3. Using the same floor plan, ask students where different rooms are. Their answers should include IX-dir, and begin from the perspective of the front door. For example, to tell where the kitchen is:

<u>   t </u> <u>   </u>   mm

ENTER, IX-dir *"down the hall and to the right"* IX-loc KITCHEN.

SIGN PRODUCTION

"Add-a-Room"

Purpose: To practice establishing a reference point, then giving a new location and identifying what's there. Also to practice correcting and confirming information.

1. Make a handout of the **floor plan of your own home** and hand out copies to the class. Tell students to describe the floor plan to you while you draw what they describe on the board.

2. First, draw just the front entranceway on the board, using the handout as a guide. Call on a student to tell you what to draw next. Students should use the following structure in their instructions:

tell location of room

(establish reference point)	(tell new location in relation to reference point)	(identify room)

For example:

<u> t </u>	<u> oo </u>	<u> cs </u>

S: ENTER, HALL(short) IX-dir *"to left"* KITCHEN "area"...

Draw exactly what the student describes. If the description is too general, make errors on purpose to force students to correct you. For example, if your kitchen is long and narrow, but the student used the sign "area" as above, draw a small square for the kitchen and ask if that's correct. Continue this until students agree you have drawn the room correctly according to the original floor plan.

3. Call on another student to describe the next room by doing the following:

    a) refer to a previously established location (i.e., the door, hallway, or kitchen)
    b) describe the new location using IX-dir
    c) identify the next room

Again, draw exactly what students describe to give them practice in correcting you.

4. After students have described the floor plan room by room, sign a brief description of the whole floor plan so that students can see how to give a general overview of the same home.

━━■BREAKAWAY

SCISSORS GAME
(see Appendix, p. 20)

Purpose: To encourage the class to function as a group and develop group cohesiveness.

THEN WHAT HAPPENED?
(see Appendix, p. 21)

Purpose: To practice signing short narratives.

INTRODUCTION

Describing the Arrangement of a Room

1. Begin by describing the classroom from the perspective of the doorway. Then, using **locative or other classifiers**, describe where:

   • seats are arranged
   • the teacher's desk is
   • the blackboards are
   • any other distinctive features of the room are located

   Use the following sentence structure, and emphasize which locative or semantic classifier (LCL or SCL) to use for different furniture:*

   describe location of furniture

_____t ENTER,	(room)	(furniture)	(classifier indicating location)

   For example:

_____t **T:** ENTER, ROOM BLACK+fs-BOARD LCL:B(palm out)*"blackboard on right"*, TABLE LCL:B(palm down)*"table in middle of room"*, CHAIR (2h)SCL:bent-V *"chairs in semi-circle"*.

   *****NOTE:** Be sure to use appropriate eye gaze and other non-manual signals to show relative distance between objects, and their relative sizes. Also be sure to describe the room according to its actual size.

(See below for which classifier to use for different pieces of furniture.)

LCL:B
(palm out)

door
window
picture

LCL:B
(palm down)

table
desk
bed

LCL:C
(palm out)

refrigerator
television
dresser

DCL:C
(palm down, sweeps)

couch
countertop

SCL:bent-V

chair

2. Take the class to another room (i.e., library, another classroom, cafeteria). Review how to describe the arrangement of the room. Then bring students back to the classroom and ask them to recall how the room is arranged. They should begin with the sign ENTER.

3. Show again the transparencies of other rooms ("Living Room," "Bedroom," "Bathroom" and "Kitchen"). Describe each room using the structure above and appropriate classifiers.

4. Point to each piece of furniture on the transparencies and have students give you the correct LCL, SCL or DCL.

5. Then sign different classifiers, and have students tell you what pieces of furniture correspond to each one.

SIGN PRODUCTION

"How Is the Room Arranged?"

Purpose: To practice locative and other classifiers. Also to practice sequencing locations by using topic-comment structure and the non-dominant hand to establish a reference point.

1. Draw a room on the board and draw a bed on the left side of the room, i.e.:

Then sign:

>   t
> **T:** BED+ROOM, ENTER, BED, LCL:B*"on left side of room"*.

Have students repeat after you.

2. Draw a table next to the bed in the picture, then demonstrate how to add information about the table by using a reference point and locative classifier. First re-establish the location of the bed with your non-dominant hand, then indicate the location of the table in relation to the bed, i.e.:

>   t
> **T:** BED (wh)LCL:B*"there"*, TABLE
> [(wh)LCL:B*"bed"*/LCL:B*"table's location in relation to the bed"*].*

Have students repeat after you.

3. Continue the procedure above, adding other pieces of furniture (dresser, chair, lamp, bookshelf, television), and using different reference points and appropriate classifiers.

4. Then describe the position of all the furniture in continuous sequence, using your non-dominant hand to hold a reference point as you describe the location of each piece of furniture.

---

*NOTE: The symbols [(wh). . ./ . . .] indicate that two signs are made at the same time: the symbol (wh) shows which sign is made with the "weak" or non-dominant hand; the gloss following the slash is the sign made with the dominant hand.

5. **Toy Furniture:** Bring some toy furniture to class. (Try to have several pieces of the same thing.) Arrange the furniture in different ways, i.e., two chairs in the corner and four chairs in the middle of the room; one chair in each of the four corners; four chairs and a coffee table in the middle. Help students develop fluency by having them describe each arrangement with appropriate classifiers.

6. Give students specific instructions on how to change the positions of the toy furniture.

7. **Magazine Pictures:** Have students bring to class magazine pictures of different rooms. Collect the pictures and put five or six in a row on the blackboard.

   Pair up students and let everyone study the pictures on the board. Then have one student in each pair mentally select one of the rooms and describe it to his/her partner. (Make sure students describe the *arrangement* of the room only — they should not refer to color.)

   The partner should identify which room was described.

8. Afterwards, put up a new set of pictures. Have students switch roles and repeat the process.

"Telling Where Objects Are"

Purpose: To develop fluency in using location vocabulary and topic-comment structure.

1. Show "The Office" transparency (see Materials Appendix, p. 33). Point to a place on the shelf and demonstrate the following structure:

[(wh)LCL:B *"surface"* **/IX-loc]**

identify a specific location in another room

			t			
KNOW	(name of room)	ENTER	IX-loc *"part of room"*	SHELF CABINET DRAWER	FIRST SECOND THIRD TOP BOTTOM MIDDLE "wave-left" "wave-right" CORNER	[(wh)LCL:B *"surface"*/ IX-loc *"location of object in relation to surface"*]*

2. Point to other places on the same transparency and call on students to practice describing the location referred to, using the structure above.

---

*NOTE: See NOTE on p. 13 explaining use of the symbols [(wh). . ./. . .] for two signs made at the same time.

3. Introduce vocabulary for the numbered items on the bottom of the transparency:

    1) DICTIONARY
    2) RUBBER+ERASE
    3) TELEPHONE+BOOK
    4) CUP
    5) TAPE
    6) SCISSORS
    7) SIGN+LANGUAGE VIDEOTAPE
    8) PLANT
    9) PICTURE+DCL*"shape of frame"*
   10) FILE+FOLD++

4. Pair off students and hand out copies of "The Office" transparency for each student to use as a worksheet (see Materials Appendix, p. 33). Tell one student in each pair to mark numbers 1 – 5 in different locations on his/her worksheet, and the other student in each pair to mark numbers 6 – 10.

Afterwards, students should describe to their partners the locations of the objects that correspond to the numbers they marked. The partners in turn mark the numbers on their worksheets. Afterwards, have students compare worksheets.

━━━━━━━━━━━━━━━━━━━━━━━━━━━━━━━━━━━ BREAKAWAY

FINGERSPELLING

Double Letters
(see Appendix, p. 22)

━━━

INTERACTION

Where's the TV Guide?

Purpose: To practice asking and giving locations, and to review quantifier vocabulary.

1. Show the "Where's the TV Guide?" transparency and introduce vocabulary for each item in the picture (see Materials Appendix, p. 34):

SHOE ICL*"polish"*	#TV+fs-GUIDE	fs-BILLS
SCISSORS	TELEPHONE+BOOK	KEY
PENNY++	SCREWDRIVER	VACUUM
STAMP	NAIL-CLIPPERS	TELEPHONE
fs-GLUE	NEEDLE+STRING (thread)	TIME+DCL*"shape of clock"*
NEWSPAPER	CANDLE	SLEEP+fs-BAG
MAGAZINE	MATCH	PICTURE BOOK (album)
BROOM	SAFETY-PIN	CAMERA
fs-NAIL	HEADACHE+MEDICINE	CALENDAR
DCL*"envelope"*	(or) fs-ASPIRIN	UMBRELLA

15

2. Write the following dialogue format on the board:

> ***Signer A:*** *ask if B has* _____ *(your assigned item)*
> **B:** *if yes, tell where you keep it*
> **A:** *ask for confirmation*
> **B:** *confirm or correct*

Demonstrate a sample dialogue:

>   q
> **A:** YOU HAVE CANDLE.
>   nod   t   cs   nod
> **B:** YES, IX-loc KITCHEN, fs-SINK, NEAR, DRAWER, IX-loc*"in drawer"*.
>   q
> **A:** NEAR fs-SINK.
>   nod
> **B:** YES.

3. Assign each student two of the items on the transparency. Then have all students circulate and follow the dialogue format, asking each other where in their homes they keep the items. Students should keep a record of the different places.

4. Call each student up front to share the answers they collected. They should summarize their findings by using quantifier vocabulary: #ALL, ALL, MOST, MANY, SOME, SEVERAL, NONE.

Ask and You Shall Receive

Purpose: To practice giving and understanding instructions for where things are located.

1. Write the following dialogue format on the board:

> ***Signer A:*** *give reason, make request*
> **B:** *agree, ask where*
> **A:** *give specific location*
> **B:** *ask for confirmation*
> **A:** *confirm or correct*
> **B:** *(go get the item)*

2. Put an object in the other room, then return. Call a student up to role play Signer B, while you sign for A and begin the dialogue. For example:

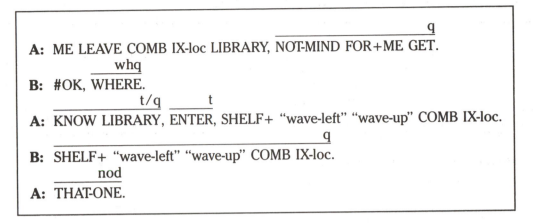

> _____ q
> **A:** ME LEAVE COMB IX-loc LIBRARY, NOT-MIND FOR+ME GET.
> ___ whq
> **B:** #OK, WHERE.
> ___ t/q ___ t
> **A:** KNOW LIBRARY, ENTER, SHELF+ "wave-left" "wave-up" COMB IX-loc.
> _____ q
> **B:** SHELF+ "wave-left" "wave-up" COMB IX-loc.
> ___ nod
> **A:** THAT-ONE.

3. Continue this with several pairs of students until they readily use the correct structure and sequence. Then divide the class into pairs and send one person from each pair to leave something in the other room. When they return, have them practice the dialogue with their partners.

Design Your Living Room

Purpose: To give students practice using location vocabulary, and practice in visualizing rooms as they describe them.

1. Divide the class into groups of three students each. Make copies of the "Design Your Living Room" worksheets (see Materials Appendix, pp. 35 – 36), cut them apart and distribute them as follows:

- give one copy of the floor plan to each group
- give a different half sheet (one set of furniture) to each person in a group

Have each person cut out his/her own set of furniture. If time permits, students can color in the furniture and add designs or patterns.

Also make a transparency of the floor plan part of the worksheet, and cut out all the furniture to use on the overhead projector.

2. Tell students in each group to pretend they are roommates, and that they must decide how to arrange their living room.

Problem: There is too much furniture to fit in the room. Students will have to decide which pieces can be used and which must be discarded.

Encourage them to discuss what goes together well, what would get the most use, what has to be discarded. Students should practice opinion vocabulary, i.e.:

GOOD+IDEA   "wave-no"   NOT+LIKE   BETTER

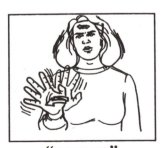

"wave no"

3. After all the groups have agreed on their room arrangement, call up one student from each group to describe the room to the whole class.*

Call on a student from *another* group to arrange the cut-outs on the overhead projector as the room is being described. Afterwards, check that the arrangements on the group's worksheet and on the overhead projector are identical. (If an overhead is not available, have the other student draw the floor plan and furniture on the blackboard.)

If students colored in their furniture, have them describe the colors and patterns they chose.

NARRATIVE PRACTICE

"Lost Shoe"

Purpose: To practice giving locations using LCLs in a narrative.

1. Show a transparency of the "Lost Shoe" picture sequence (see Materials Appendix, p. 37). Tell a story about the boy looking for his shoe. Begin by telling how he discovered the shoe was missing, in which rooms and what specific places he looked, and how he found the shoe.

   • use GONE to indicate the missing shoe
   • use SCL:1 to show the boy moving from room to room
   • use LOOK-AT to show where the boy looked (i.e., under, in, over)
   • use NONE to indicate the shoe was not there
   • use role shifting to show actions of the boy and parents when looking in different places
   • use DISGUSTED as the final reaction after finding it in the dog house

2. Afterwards, ask both general and specific questions about the story. Students should be able to tell you both where the boy and his parents looked (using LCLs) and the general sequence of the story.

3. Pair up students and hand out copies of the "Lost Shoe" illustration. Tell students to change the order of events by re-numbering the picture frames.

   Each student should tell his/her partner another version of the "Lost Shoe" story, with a new beginning and a different order of events. The partner is to number the picture frames according to the new version.

---

*NOTE: Make sure students discuss the room arrangement using a "real-world" reference frame. That is, they should talk about the room and furniture as if they were actual size.

4. Tell students a story about your experience losing something and searching for it (i.e., keys, eyeglasses, bills, phone number, tickets for a show). When appropriate, introduce or review the vocabulary:

BE-LOST   LOOK-FOR   FIND

5. Write the following on the board:

> *Tell a story about losing something, using this narrative sequence:*
> * *how you realized it was missing*
> * *where you looked (include several different places, and describe specific locations within the places)*
> * *how you finally found it (and your reaction)*

Have students follow the instructions on the board, telling their own stories about misplacing something and searching for it.

STUDENT VIDEOTEXT AND WORKBOOK

1. Make sure students complete the video-interactive and other activities for this unit, either in class or for homework. Also assign the Culture/Language Notes for this unit.

End of Unit 13

APPENDIX

SCISSORS GAME

1. Have the whole class sit in a circle, and make sure everyone can see each other. Write on the board:

> *Object of the game: guess the rule*

Start the game by passing a pair of scissors to the person on your left. Make sure you follow the rule, but don't tell it to the class! The rule is simple:

- if your legs are crossed, you must pass the scissors *closed*

RIGHT   WRONG

- if your legs are not crossed, you must pass the scissors *open*

RIGHT   WRONG

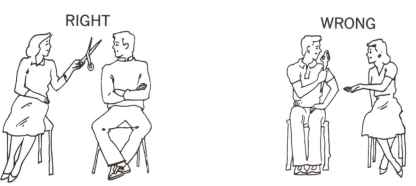

Have the next person pass the scissors: if his/her legs are crossed and s/he passes it closed, say that s/he did it right; if his/her legs are not crossed and s/he passes it closed, say that s/he did it wrong.

2. Continue going around the room, with each person passing the scissors and you saying whether it was right or wrong.

When most of the players think they have guessed the rule, call on a student to explain it. Continue this until someone can explain the rule correctly.

Variation: When a student says s/he knows the rule, have him/her take your place, telling other students whether they passed it correctly or not. In this way you can tell whether the student understands the rule. Then as others say they know the rule, have them take the place of the leader. Continue this until most students say they know the rule. Then call on someone to explain it to the others.

3. Encourage students to interact, making comments and asking questions throughout the game. Afterwards, have them discuss their different theories, and the process of figuring out the rule.

THEN WHAT HAPPENED?

1. Divide the class into groups of four students each. Hand out a different story from the "Then What Happened?" picture sequences to each student in a group (see Materials Appendix, pp. 38 – 41).

   Write the following on the board:

Imagine you are the person in the picture sequence. Tell a story that includes:

Introduction

- *tell when this occurred*
- *tell what you were going to do*

Body

- *describe the sequence of activities*
- *include your feelings about some of the activities*

Closing

- *tell your surprise ending, and your reaction*

Have each student develop a narrative based on his/her picture sequence, and sign it to the others in the group. Students should tell their story in the first person, that is, as if they themselves were the person in the picture sequence.

2. Afterwards, ask questions about the stories, i.e.:

   - how would they build a table differently next time
   - how did they feel about cleaning the fish
   - what was the reason for baking a cake

FINGERSPELLING

Double Letters

1. Fingerspell the following words and have students write them down. Note that all the words have double letters.

fingerspelled names

fs-BOBBY	fs-BILLY	fs-BONNIE	fs-BARRY
fs-DEBBIE	fs-ELLEN	fs-CONNIE	fs-HARRY
fs-LIBBY	fs-HOLLY	fs-DANNY	fs-LARRY
fs-BIFF	fs-JILL	fs-DONNA	fs-CASSIE
fs-CLIFF	fs-POLLY	fs-JENNIFER	fs-JESSE
fs-JEFF	fs-SALLY	fs-JENNY	fs-BETTY
fs-TIFFANY	fs-SHELLY	fs-KENNETH	fs-JEANETTE
fs-PEGGY	fs-WILLIAM	fs-LYNN	fs-LYNNETTE
fs-TWIGGY	fs-SAMMY	fs-WINNIE	fs-PATTY
fs-NIKKI	fs-TAMMY		

fingerspelled numbers

fs-MILLION	fs-BILLION	fs-TRILLION	fs-ZILLION

other possible fingerspelled words

fs-KIBBLE	fs-HILL	fs-CHANNEL	fs-CLASSIC
fs-LUCCA	fs-KILL	fs-INNING	fs-SASSY
fs-BEEF	fs-KILLED	fs-COOL	fs-BATTER
fs-BEER	fs-WALL	fs-DOOR	fs-BATTLE
fs-FREE	fs-WELL	fs-NOODLE	fs-CATTLE
fs-SEED	fs-WILL	fs-HIPPIE	fs-COTTON
fs-TWEET	fs-WILLOW	fs-PUPPY	fs-LITTER
fs-WEED	fs-COMMON	fs-YUPPIE	fs-SAVVY
fs-BALL	fs-COMMUNE	fs-BURRITO	fs-PIZZA
fs-DULL	fs-IMMUNE	FIRST fs-CLASS	

2. Fingerspell the words again, but this time have students repeat the words after you. Make sure they fingerspell the double letters with a short sideways sweep from left to right.

3. Now fingerspell the words in ASL sentences. Have students either repeat or write down only the fingerspelled word.

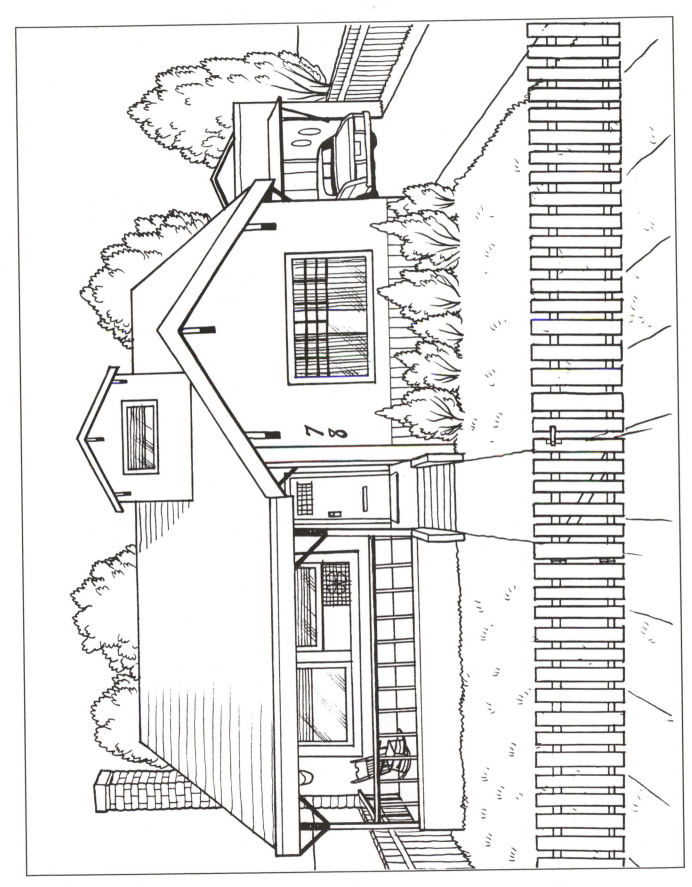

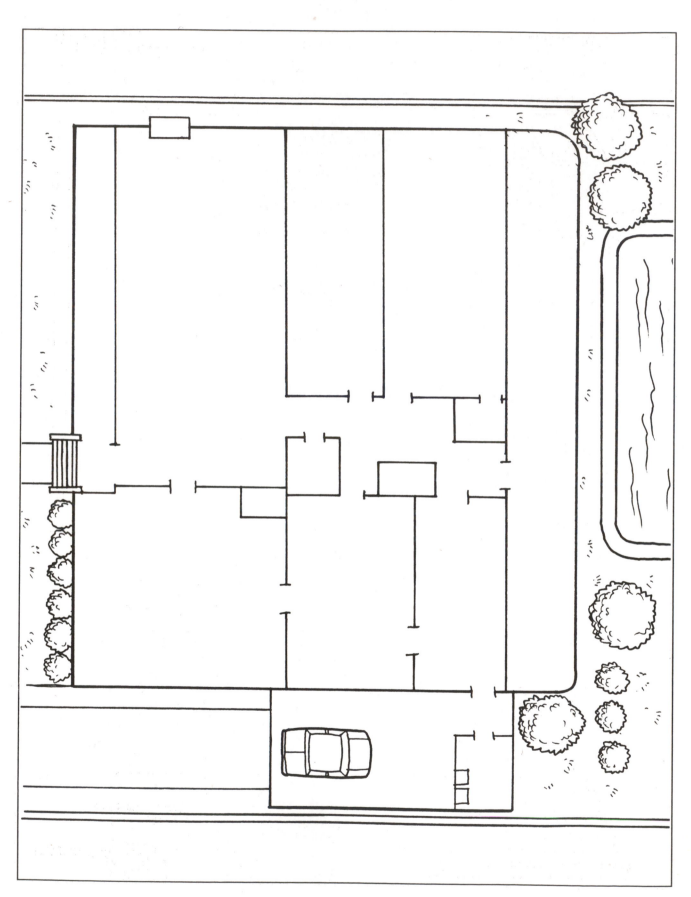

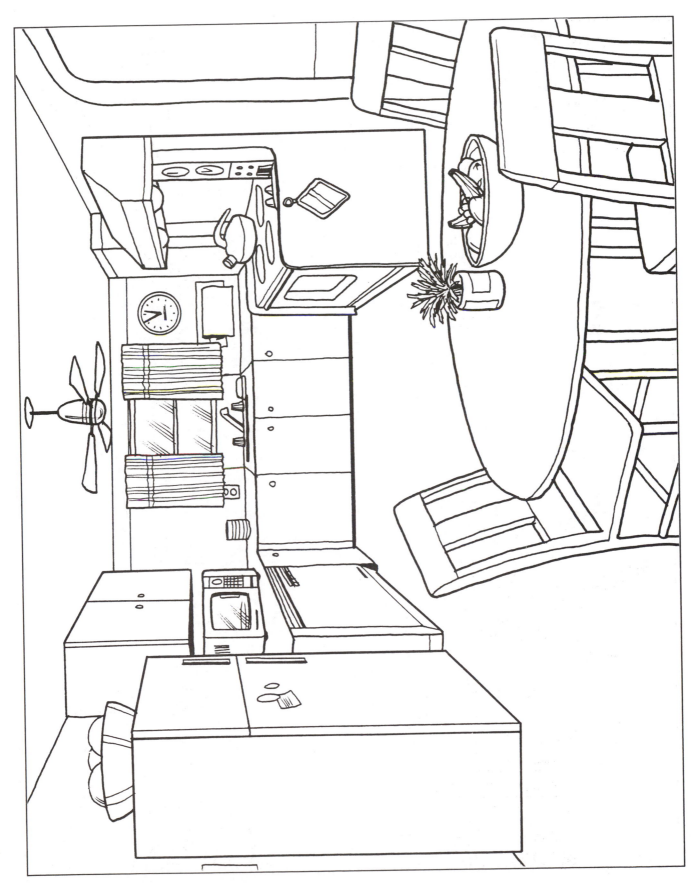

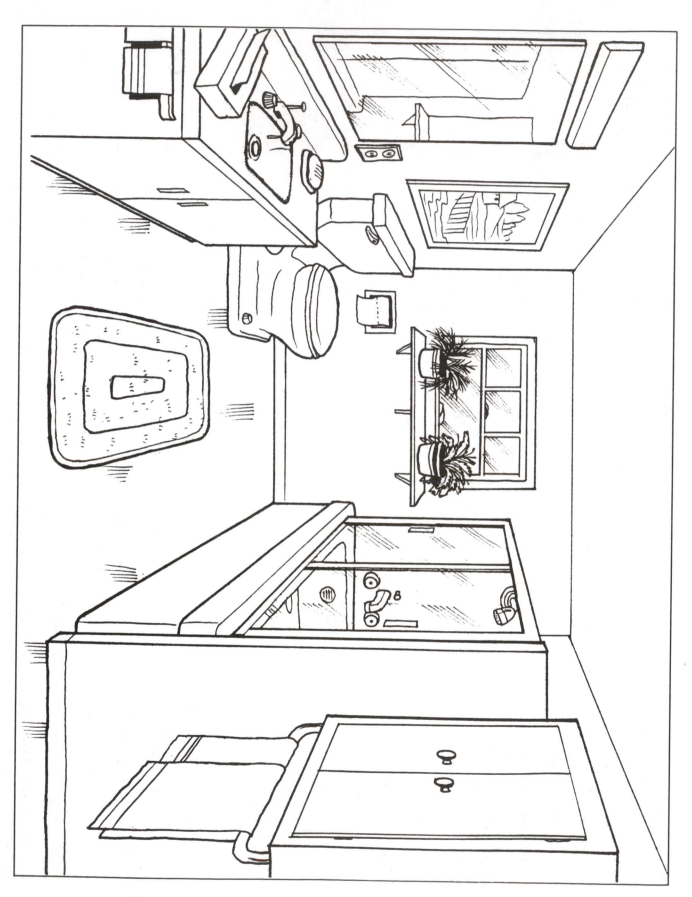

	You	Student 2	Student 3	Student 4

Student 1: The Home in General

1) kind of housing (apartment, dorm, condo, etc.)

2) number of stories

3) color of building and trim

4) color of front door

5) size of yard

   — is it fenced?

6) is there a swimming pool?

   — garage?

   — attic?

   — basement?

   — deck or porch?

   — elevator?

7) number of bedrooms

   — bathrooms

8) type of telephone(s)

   — in which rooms?

9) is there a shower, bathtub or both?

10) is there a shower curtain or door?

	Student 1	You	Student 3	Student 4

Student 2: Living Room

1) size of living room

   — what color?

2) number of windows

   — what kind?

   — type of window covering?

3) is there a fireplace?

   — a ceiling fan?

   — a TV or stereo?

are there pictures on the wall?

4) is there a rug or carpeting?

   — what color?

5) what kind of furniture is there?

6) number of lamps

   — what kind?

7) are there plants?

   — where are they located?

8) last time the walls were painted?

Student 3: Bedroom

	Student 1	Student 2	You	Student 4
1) size of bedroom				
— what color?				
2) is there an adjoining bathroom?				
3) number of closets				
— what size?				
— what kind of closet doors?				
4) is there a mirror?				
— how big?				
— where is it located?				
5) number of windows				
— what kind?				
— type of window covering?				
6) what kind of bedroom furniture?				
— size of bed				
— color of bedspread				
7) what do you have up on the walls?				

	Student 1	Student 2	Student 3	You

Student 4: Kitchen

1) size of kitchen

   — what color?

2) what kind of refrigerator? (i.e., separate freezer, positions of doors)

   — what color?

3) electric or gas stove

4) is there a microwave oven?

   — dishwasher?

5) are the stove, refrigerator and dishwasher all the same color?

6) is there a separate dining area?

7) is there a window above the sink?

   — is it a double sink?

   — what kind of faucet (hot and cold combined?)

8) is there a laundry room near the kitchen?

9) number of kitchen cabinets

   — what color?

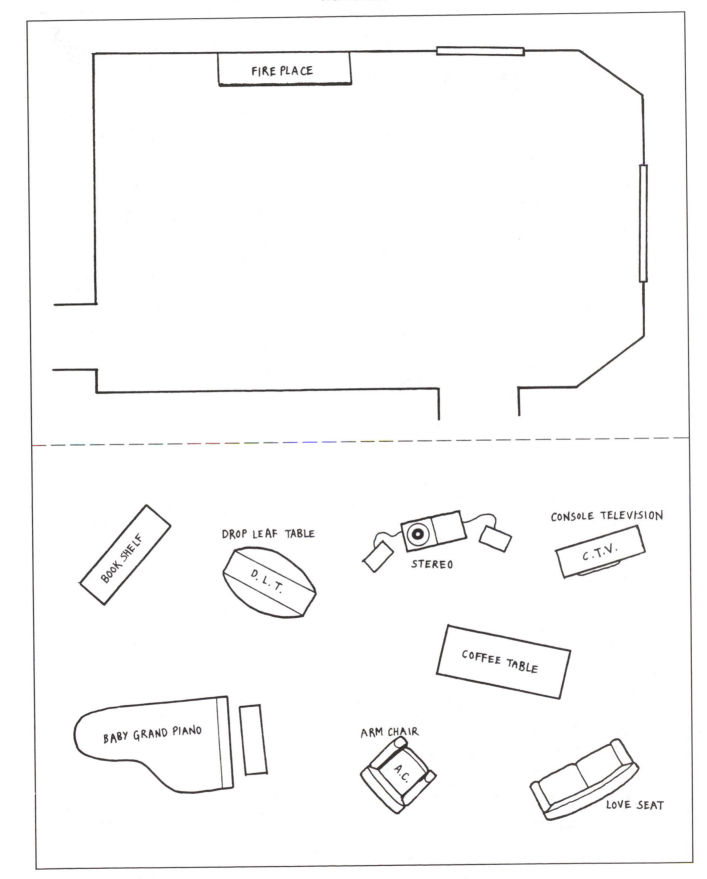

FIRE PLACE

BOOK SHELF

DROP LEAF TABLE

D. L. T.

STEREO

CONSOLE TELEVISION

C.T.V.

COFFEE TABLE

BABY GRAND PIANO

ARM CHAIR

A.C.

LOVE SEAT

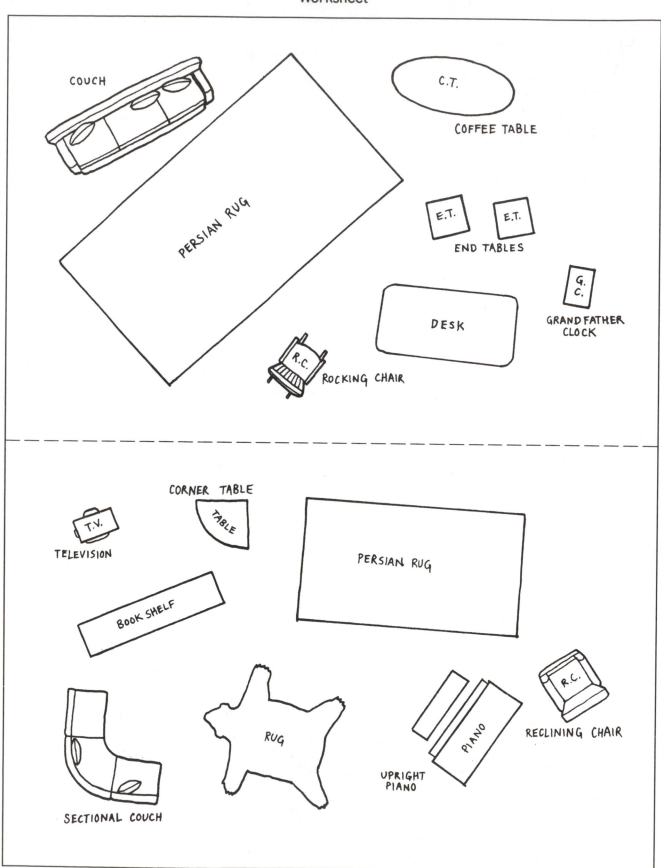

COUCH

C.T.

COFFEE TABLE

PERSIAN RUG

E.T.

E.T.

END TABLES

G. C.

GRANDFATHER CLOCK

DESK

R.C.

ROCKING CHAIR

CORNER TABLE

TABLE

T.V.

TELEVISION

PERSIAN RUG

BOOK SHELF

R.C.

RUG

PIANO

UPRIGHT PIANO

RECLINING CHAIR

SECTIONAL COUCH

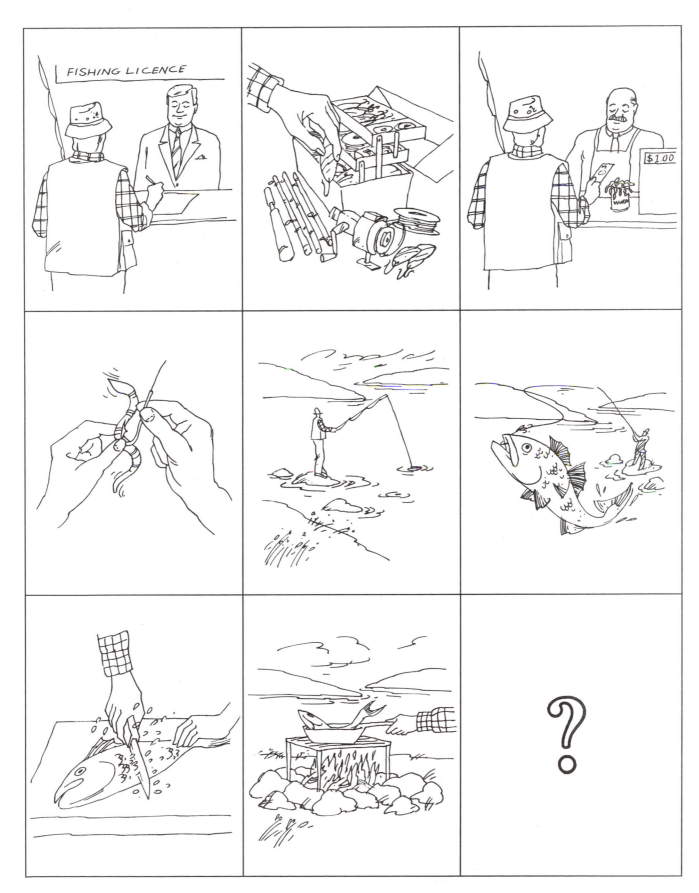

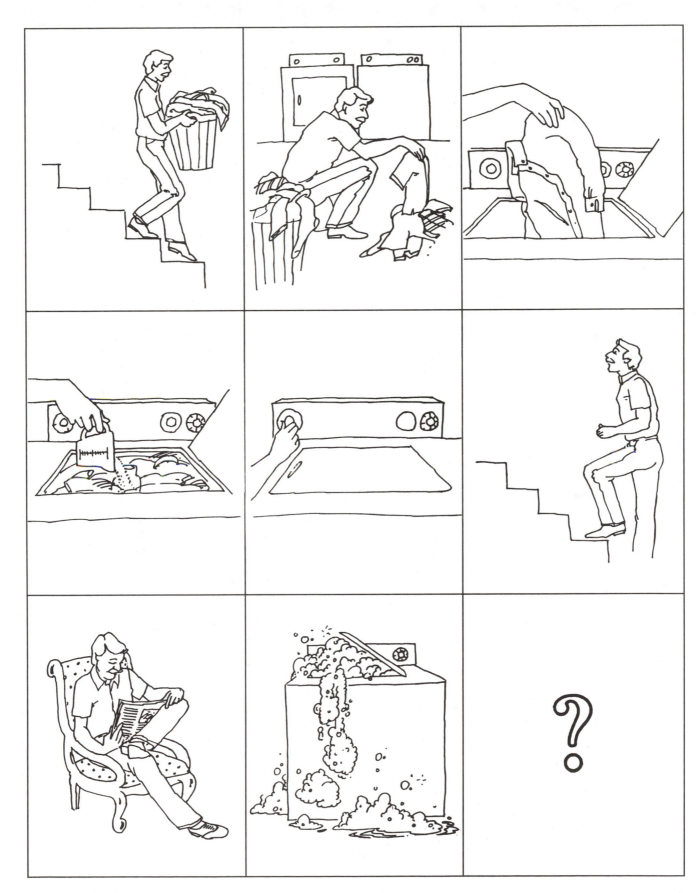

UNIT 14

COMPLAINING, MAKING SUGGESTIONS AND REQUESTS
OVERVIEW

DIALOGUE FORMAT:

Signer A: give reason, make request
    B: decline, explain why, suggest another time/solution
A and B: negotiate until you agree on the best time/solution

SAMPLE DIALOGUE:

Signer A: [MY] DAUGHTER SCHOOL TELEPHONE ME, TELL-TO-*me* DAUGHTER SICK, fs-RASH DCL:5*"all over body"*, SCRATCHING++. ME THINK BETTER GO-AWAY HOME (2h)LOOK-AT++.

<u>   q</u>
NOT-MIND US-TWO EAT POSTPONE TOMORROW.
              <u>grimace</u>   <u>t/q</u>   <u>neg</u>

    B: REAL/TRUE++, "wow". TOMORROW, ME CAN'T.
                           <u>nod</u>   <u>q</u>
STUCK WORK. FUTURE THURSDAY BETTER, "well".

        <u>q</u>
    A: THURSDAY. FINE++.

VOCABULARY:

ailments	suggestions	time signs: recurring	complaints
HAVE-PAIN	FINISH	EVERY-MORNING	SICK-OF
HAVE-CRAMP	WHY+NOT	EVERY-AFTERNOON	TEND-TO
COUGH	SHOULD	EVERY-NIGHT	ALWAYS
HAVE-COLD		EVERYDAY	problems with pets
HAVE-SORE-THROAT	**remedies**	EVERY-WEEK	problems with children
SCRATCHING	MEDICINE	EVERY-MONTH	problems with
FEEL-TIRED	TAKE-PILL	EVERY-HOUR	roommates/spouse
NOT+FEEL+GOOD	SPOON-IN-SYRUP	UP-TILL-NOW OFTEN	problems with neighbors
DCL:bent-5*"swollen part of body"*	ICL*"use dropper"*		
	BCL*"rub on"*	**time signs: continuous**	**requests**
CAN'T+SLEEP+SCL:V *"toss and turn in bed"*	CALL-BY PHONE DOCTOR	ALL-MORNING	NOT-MIND
HAVE-UPSET-STOMACH	LIE-DOWN REST	ALL-AFTERNOON	POSTPONE
(2h)VOMIT		ALL-NIGHT	PREPONE
FEEL-DIZZY	**empathize**	ALL-DAY	SHOW-TO-*person*
HAVE-DIARRHEA	"pshaw"	ALL-WEEK	TELL-TO-*person*
RED "area of body"	AWFUL	ALL-MONTH	ASK-TO-*person*
fs-RASH	"wow"	ALL-HOUR	CALL-BY-PHONE-*person*
FEEL-SORE	KNOW+		GIVE-TO-*person*
FEEL+LOUSY		**other**	INFORM-*person*
		STUCK	SUMMON-*person*
		BETTER	PARTICIPATE
			HOLD-DOWN*"place"*
		clock numbers	ALL-RIGHT
		commonly fingerspelled words	PERMIT

SENTENCE STRUCTURES:

make suggestion

		q
FINISH	(remedy)	YOU

		q
WHY+NOT SHOULD	(remedy)	"well"

complain about others

(pet/person)	TEND-TO ALWAYS	[(time sign)]	(actions)	[ME] SICK-OF

ME SICK-OF	(pet/person)	(actions),	"pshaw"

request help with tasks

(give reason),	NOT-MIND	GO-TO HELP	q (task) ICL"*task with tool/utensil*" PICK-UP (person/thing) GET (object) (object) BRING-TO (place) WASH"*object*"

request time change

(explain situation),	NOT-MIND CAN	(event)	POSTPONE PREPONE	q (other time)

make indirect request

NOT-MIND YOU	ASK-TO-*person* TELL-TO-*person* INFORM-*person* SUMMON-*person*	(name)	q (object) GIVE-TO-*me* CALL-BY-PHONE-*me* TELL-TO-*me* INFORM-*me* SHOW-TO-*me* COME-TO SEE ME

ask for permission

| [(give reason)], | NOT-MIND ME BORROW
PERMIT ME USE | (money or object) ___q |
| | NOT-MIND
ALL-RIGHT ME
CAN ME
#OK
PERMIT | (2h)SCL:V"*two people trade places*" ___q
TAKE-FROM"*place*" (object)
(object) MOVE-TO"*place*" |

GRAMMAR:

recurring time signs: EVERY-(time sign)
continuous time signs: ALL-(time sign)
temporal aspect: recurring
                continuous
inflecting verbs
role shifting
conditional sentences

CONVERSATION STRATEGIES:

asking for clarification
clarifying
agreeing
declining
hedging

SIGN ILLUSTRATIONS:

HAVE-UPSET-STOMACH (see p. 45)
UP-TILL-NOW (see p. 45)
GO-AWAY (see p. 46)
SICK-OF (see p. 50)
TOO-CLEAN (see p. 51)
SPEND-MONEY-FAST (see p. 51)
LEAVE-ALONE (see p. 51)
ECL"*odor from body*" (see p. 51)
COMMUTE (see p. 51)
BE-BEHIND-IN (see p. 51)
NOSY (see p. 51)
NOT-MIND (see p. 54)
POUR-MONEY-IN (see p. 54)
PREPONE (see p. 54)
CALL-BY-PHONE (see p. 55)
HOLD-DOWN"*place*" (see p. 55)
FIRST-*thumb* (see p. 61)

MATERIALS:

"Ailments" transparency
"Inflected Forms" transparency
"Situations" transparency
"Asking Permission" transparency
Role Play Cards
"One Fine Day" Summary

blank cards
airline flight schedules or other timetables
book: *One Fine Day* by Nonny Hogrogian

44

INTRODUCTION

Identify the Ailment

1. Show the "Ailments" transparency (see Materials Appendix, p. 66).

Introduce the following vocabulary by signing narratives about people with the different ailments:

HAVE-UPSET-STOMACH

a) HAVE-PAIN*

b) HAVE-CRAMP

c) COUGH

d) HAVE-COLD

e) HAVE-SORE-THROAT

f) SCRATCHING

g) FEEL-TIRED

h) DCL:bent-5 *"swollen part of body"*

i) CAN'T+SLEEP+SCL:V *"toss and turn"*

j) HAVE-UPSET-STOMACH

k) (2h)VOMIT

l) FEEL-DIZZY

m) HAVE-DIARRHEA

n) RED "area of body"

n) fs-RASH

o) FEEL-SORE

Include the following vocabulary in your narratives as well:

p) NOT+FEEL+GOOD

p) FEEL+LOUSY

Sample narrative about your son having an upset stomach (illustration j):

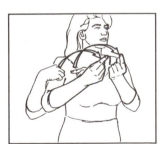

UP-TILL-NOW

> **T:** MY SON, NOT GO-TO SCHOOL, UP-TILL-NOW TWO-DAYS. IX
>   _____neg
> **NOT+FEEL+GOOD** <rs:son BCL*"hands on stomach indicating*
> *indigestion",* "wave" MOM IX-loc*"stomach",* **HAVE-UPSET-**
> **STOMACH**>. ME <rs:narrator BCL*"tell him to relax"*
> MEDICINE SPOON-IN-SYRUP>. NOW LITTLE-BIT BETTER++.

After signing the narrative, ask students to identify which illustration on the transparency matches what you signed. Then introduce the signs for that illustration, i.e.:

            neg
NOT+FEEL+GOOD, HAVE-UPSET-STOMACH.

---

*NOTE: The sign HAVE-PAIN should be signed in the affected area of the face or head. However, for other parts of the body, the sign HAVE-PAIN should be signed in neutral space followed by pointing to the affected area of the body.

2. Continue the same sequence for the other illustrations on the transparency.

Other sample narratives (illustrations i and n):

> **T:** ME FEEL+LOUSY. PAST+NIGHT ME DRINK++ COFFEE. WRONG ALL-NIGHT WIDE-AWAKE **CAN'T SLEEP SCL:V***"toss and turn"*. ME DRINK WARM MILK. FINALLY SLEEP TIME+4 EARLY-MORNING.
>
> AWFUL. PAST+SATURDAY MY FRIEND US-TWO GO-TO TREE++ WALK. !ENJOY!. ARRIVE HOME, WRONG DCL*"itch on chest"*. ICL*"lift up my shirt"* **RED+"chest area"** fs-RASH SCRATCHING. PINK MEDICINE BCL*"rub on"*. NOW MELT-AWAY.

SIGN PRODUCTION

"Making Suggestions about Health"

Purpose: To practice vocabulary and sentence structures for complaining about physical conditions, making suggestions, and responding.

1. Write the following dialogue format on the board:

> ***Signer A:*** *express concern*
> **B:** *complain about present condition*
> **A:** *make suggestion*
> **B:** *respond*

Role play both Signers A and B:

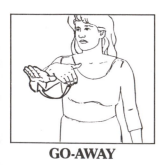

GO-AWAY

>   q
> **Signer A:** YOU FEEL #OK.
>   t
> **B:** TODAY ALL-AFTERNOON, ME FEEL+LOUSY, FEEL-TIRED, HAVE-SORE-THROAT, EYES HAVE-PAIN THUMB-loc*"back"* fs-BACK FEEL-SORE.
>   whq
> **A:** WHY+NOT GO-AWAY HOME.
>   nod
> **B:** GOOD+IDEA.

2. Call on students to role play Signer B. Tell them to complain about various physical conditions, while you give suggestions as Signer A.

Introduce the following sentence structure for Signer A (line 3):

make suggestion

			q
FINISH	SEE DOCTOR		YOU
	MEDICINE	ICL"*use dropper*" TAKE-PILL SPOON-IN-SYRUP BCL"*rub on*"	

	concern/q	
WHY+NOT*	CALL-BY-PHONE DOCTOR GO-AWAY HOME	

		concern/q	q
SHOULD	[TRY] MEDICINE	SPOON-IN-SYRUP TAKE-PILL BCL"*rub on*" ICL"*use dropper*"	"well"
	LIE-DOWN, REST		

3. Reverse roles: you be Signer B complaining about different ailments, and have students be Signer A, making suggestions that use the sentence structure above.

4. Demonstrate phrases for Signer B's **responses**:

GOOD+IDEA.

RIGHT YOU.

        nod
[YES,] ME SHOULD.

#OK, ME TRY.

    nod   neg
ME FINISH. NOT+HELP.

    grimace   neg
(shake head) CAN'T.

5. Have students practice the dialogue in pairs.

6. Demonstrate varying **degrees of complaints**: sign the dialogue again, but for Signer B's complaint, express more frustration (bigger, stronger, repeated signs, with more emphatic facial expressions).

---

*NOTE: WHY+NOT is used to suggest an idea, and can be signed with either yes/no or wh-question non-manual markers, depending on the situation. The wh-question form is used in familiar situations when suggesting a solution; raised eyebrows are often used when suggesting an activity.

"Complaining About Feeling Sick"

Purpose: To practice signing inflected and uninflected forms of ailment-verb signs, with corresponding time signs.

1. Write the following dialogue format on the board:

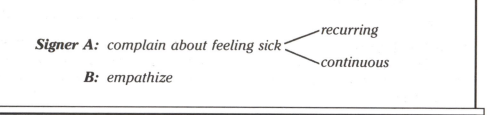

Introduce or review the following time signs:

recurring	continuous*
EVERY-MORNING	ALL-MORNING
EVERY-AFTERNOON	ALL-AFTERNOON
EVERY-NIGHT	ALL-NIGHT
EVERYDAY	ALL-DAY
EVERY-WEEK	ALL-WEEK
EVERY-MONTH	ALL-MONTH
EVERY-HOUR	ALL-HOUR
UP-TILL-NOW (one of above)	UP-TILL-NOW (one of above)
UP-TILL-NOW OFTEN	

2. Role play the dialogue twice, once for recurring and once for continuous, using a different form of the same verb each time:

> **T:** (point to recurring, then sign for A and B)
>
> **A:** EVERY-MORNING ME VOMIT++.
>   <u>concern</u>
> **B:** REAL/TRUE++.
>
> **T:** (point to continuous, then sign)
>
> **A:** ALL-MORNING ME VOMIT-*cont.*
>   <u>concern</u>
> **B:** REAL/TRUE++.

---

*NOTE: The movement of these signs is different from the basic time signs: they begin with a "hold", then sweep with a slower motion and with tension held throughout. This indicates the *duration* of time (i.e., "all week" instead of "one week").

Repeat Signer A's complaint using another verb sign:

> **T:** (point to recurring, then sign) EVERY-MORNING MOTHER fs-FOOT
> DCL:claw *"swollen foot"*++.
>
> (point to continuous, then sign) ALL-DAY MOTHER fs-FOOT
> <u>   puff cheeks   </u>
> DCL:claw *"swollen foot"-hold.*

3. Show the "Inflected Forms" transparency (see Materials Appendix, p. 67). Show how the form of the verb sign may change to agree with the time concept expressed, i.e., whether it happened once, was recurring, or was continuous. For example:

   - point to the picture of someone vomiting and show the uninflected form VOMIT
   - then point to "repetitive" and show how the sign is repeated to mean "vomit again and again"
   - then point to "circular" and show how the sign has a circular motion to mean "vomiting continuously"
   - continue for each ailment illustrated

   After introducing all the sign forms, go back and point to either "recurring" or "continuous" on the dialogue format, give the uninflected form of an ailment sign, then ask students how to sign the inflected form.

4. Call two students up front, point to one of the ailment pictures on the transparency, and give a time sign from the lists on p. 48. Instruct Signer A to tell about feeling ill.

   After the students satisfactorily role play the dialogue, repeat the whole procedure with other students.

INTRODUCTION

Complaining About Others and Making Suggestions

1. Write on the board:

> *making complaints about: pets*
> *children*
> *roommates/spouse*
> *neighbors*

2. Point to "pets" on the board and begin by stating some complaints people usually have about pets, then have students add other common complaints, i.e.:

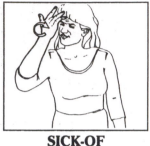

SICK-OF

> <u> t </u>   <u> rhet </u>
> **T:** PET, #DOG, CAT, PEOPLE SICK-OF "what", IX-*thumb* #DOG
> TEND-TO BARK++, IX-*index* CAT ALWAYS YELL++,
>   <u> whq </u>
> IX-*middle* "what".
>
> **S:** (give examples)

Suggested vocabulary to complain about pets:

BITE-ON++*	LICK-ON++*
COME-TO++	(2h)SCL:V"*jump on*"++
fs-HAIR FALL-OUT++	BARK++
YELL++	

Explain that the verbs in complaint structures are usually signed with "recurring" aspect inflection.

3. Point to "children" and follow the same procedure.

>   <u> rhet </u>
> **T:** CHILDREN, PEOPLE SICK-OF "what", IX-*thumb* CHILDREN TEND-TO
> SPILL++, IX-*index* CHILDREN ALWAYS PHYSICAL-FIGHT++,
>   <u> whq </u>
> IX-*middle*, "what".
>
> **S:** (give examples)

Suggested vocabulary to complain about children:

SPILL++	TAKE-FROM++
BE-LOST++	TATTLE++
STEAL++	CRY++
NOISE++	YELL++
BREAK++	LIE++
AFRAID-*char***	QUARREL++
COMPLAIN-*char***	MISCHIEVOUS-*char***
PHYSICAL-FIGHT++	(2h)alt.DROP++
FORGET++	

*****NOTE:** Be sure students' mouth movements correspond with the movement of these signs, i.e., the tongue should move in conjunction with the fingers in the sign LICK-ON++.

******NOTE:** The suffix "-*char*" indicates the verb modulation showing "characteristic" behavior or trait.

4. Point to "roommates/spouse" and follow the same procedure.

TOO-CLEAN

>   <u>rhet</u>
>
> **T:** PEOPLE COMPLAIN ABOUT HUSBAND, WIFE, ROOMMATE "what",
> IX-*thumb* ROOMMATE TEND-TO BORROW-FROM-*me*++, IX-*index*
>   <u>whq</u>
> ROOMMATE ALWAYS COMPLAIN++, IX-*middle* "what".
>
> **S:** (give examples)

Suggested vocabulary to complain about roommates/spouse:

FORGET++	LEAVE-ALONE++
[ALWAYS] GO-OUT++	COMPLAIN++
LATE++	TAKE-FROM-*me*++
BORROW-FROM-*me*++	USE-*cont* MY (object)
TOO-CLEAN++	ECL*"odor from body"*++
OVERSLEEP++	LATE++
TEMPTED++	(2h)EAT++
BUY++	COMMUTE++ BATHROOM
SPEND-MONEY-FAST++	BE-BROKE++
WORRY-*char*	BE-BEHIND-IN++
SMOKE-CIGARETTE++	WORK-*cont*
BITE-NAILS++	

SPEND-MONEY-FAST

5. Point to "neighbors" and follow the same procedure.

LEAVE-ALONE

>   <u>rhet</u>
>
> **T:** SOMETIMES PEOPLE SICK-OF NEIGHBOR WHY, IX-*thumb*
> NEIGHBOR ALWAYS NOISE++, IX-*index* NEIGHBOR TEND-TO
>   <u>whq</u>
> NOSY++, IX-*middle*, "what".
>
> **S:** (give examples)

ECL*"odor from body"*

Suggested vocabulary to complain about neighbors:

NOISE++
NOSY++
COMPLAIN++
BOTHER-*me*++
COME-TO++
GOSSIP++

NOSY

BE-BEHIND-IN

COMMUTE

SIGN PRODUCTION

"I Can't Stand It Anymore!"

Purpose: To practice complaint vocabulary about habitual behaviors, as well as vocabulary for empathizing and making suggestions.

1. Write the following dialogue format on the board:

> **Signer A:** *complain about: pet*
> *children*
> *roommate*
> *spouse*
> *brother or sister*
> *neighbor*
> **B:** *empathize, then suggest*
> **A:** *respond*

2. Demonstrate a sample dialogue about a roommate. Role play both Signers A and B.

Sample dialogue:

> **A:** MY ROOMMATE ALWAYS FORGET++ ICL*"flush"* TOILET, SICK-OF.
> **B:** "pshaw". WHY+NOT ICL*"tack on"* DCL*"sign"* PLEASE ICL*"flush"*.
>   <u>nod</u>
> **A:** GOOD+IDEA.

3. Point to "complain" and demonstrate the following sentence structures:

complain about others

(pet/person)	TEND-TO ALWAYS	[(time sign)]	(actions)	[ME] SICK-OF

ME SICK-OF	(pet/person)	(actions),	"pshaw"

Go around the room asking students to come up with a complaint for each topic on the board. Make sure they follow either of the sentence structures above.

Sample complaints:

MY #DOG TEND-TO EVERY-MORNING (2h)SCL:V*"jump on"*++, LICK-ON-*face*++, SICK-OF.
ME SICK-OF ROOMMATE USE-*cont* MY SHAMPOO, "pshaw".

4. Point to "empathize" on the board and demonstrate other phrases for empathizing:

$$\overline{\text{stress}}$$
"pshaw"

$$\overline{\text{nod}}$$
KNOW+ "pshaw"

$$\overline{\text{grimace}}$$
"pshaw" AWFUL

$$\overline{\text{grimace}}$$
"wow"

5. Point to "suggest" on the dialogue format. Review these three phrases for suggesting:

$$\overline{\phantom{\text{FINISH... YO}}\text{q}}$$
FINISH... YOU

$$\overline{\phantom{\text{WHY+NOT...}}\text{q}}$$
WHY+NOT... "well"

$$\overline{\phantom{\text{SHOULD..}}\text{q}}$$
SHOULD... "well"

6. Call two students up front and have them sign a dialogue based on the dialogue format on the board.

7. Divide the class into groups of three. One student should complain, while the other two empathize and make suggestions. Then they should all switch roles and continue with another complaint.

■ B R E A K A W A Y

AT THE GARAGE
(see Appendix, p. 64)

Purpose: To encourage students to use mime, descriptive, instrument and element classifiers, and correct spatial reference as they communicate specific needs. This will help students develop alternative strategies for expressing things they do not know how to sign, *without* resorting to fingerspelling.

FAST FORWARD
(see Appendix, p. 65)

Purpose: To encourage students to feel comfortable using different signing sizes or manners with appropriate facial expressions.

FINGERSPELLING

Commonly Fingerspelled Words
(see Appendix, p. 65)

INTRODUCTION

Making Requests

1. Write on the board the following list of reasons for making a request:

> *Reasons for request*
> *need help with tasks*
> *need to change date or time of plan*
> *want to ask favor of a third person*
> *want to join a group*
> *need someone to hold your place*

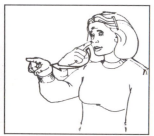

NOT-MIND

Point to "need help with tasks" on the board and show Situation 1 on the "Situations" transparency (see Materials Appendix, p. 68). Demonstrate a request for that situation, i.e.:

>   <u>   stress   </u>   q
> **T:** ME BUSY++ WORK DCL*"big pile"*; **NOT-MIND** PAPER COPY++.

Introduce the sign NOT-MIND. Explain that it is one way to make a request.

POUR-MONEY-IN

2. Show Situation 2A on the transparency and point to "need to change date or time of plan" on the board. Demonstrate a sample request for that situation, i.e.:

> **T:** ONE-WEEK-PAST CAR BREAK-DOWN, ME POUR-MONEY-IN. NOW,
>   q
> ME BROKE. NOT-MIND SKIING **POSTPONE** FUTURE+MONTH.

Introduce the sign POSTPONE.

PREPONE

3. Show Situation 2B on the transparency and point again to "need to change date or time of plan" on the board. Demonstrate a request for the situation:

> **T:** JUST-NOW MOTHER+FATHER TELEPHONE TELL-TO-*me* THEY-TWO
> FLY-TO*"here"* STAY ALL-TWO-WEEKS. REMEMBER FUTURE FRIDAY
>   t
> NIGHT US-TWO EAT GO-OUT, NOT-MIND **PREPONE** WEDNESDAY,
>   q
> THURSDAY NIGHT.

Introduce the sign PREPONE.

4. Point to "want to ask favor of a third person" on the board and show Situation 3 on the transparency. Demonstrate a sample request for that situation, i.e.:

> <u>   t/q   </u>
> **T:** KNOW++ fs-MAUREEN... "well" PAST+MONTH IX <u>BORROW-FROM-*me*</u>
> MY fs-THAI COOK BOOK. NOW ME NEED BOOK. <u>NOT-MIND YOU</u>
> <u>   q   </u>
> TELL-TO-*her* BOOK *she*-GIVE-TO-*me*.

Introduce or review the following request vocabulary, inflecting for:

- me to you
- you to third person
- third person to me

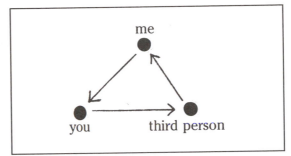

ASK-TO-*person*   GIVE-TO-*person*

TELL-TO-*person*   SHOW-TO-*person*

INFORM-*person*   COME-TO [SEE (person)]

SUMMON-*person*   GO-TO [SEE (person)]

CALL-BY-PHONE-*person*

CALL-BY-PHONE

5. Point to "want to join a group" on the board and show Situation 4 on the transparency. Demonstrate how to sign a request for that situation, i.e.:

> <u>   surprised   </u>   <u>   q </u>
> **T:** HELLO, SURPRISE SEE-*you*... NOT-MIND ME **PARTICIPATE**.

Introduce the sign PARTICIPATE.

6. Point to "need someone to hold your place" on the board and show Situation 5 on the transparency. Demonstrate a request for that situation:

> <u>   q </u>
> **T:** "snap fingers" ME FORGET BUTTER. NOT-MIND YOU **HOLD-DOWN** *"place"*.
> ME GO-TO, COME-TO *"here"*.

HOLD-DOWN *"place"*

Introduce the sign HOLD-DOWN.

SIGN PRODUCTION

"Would You Do Me a Favor?"

Purpose: To practice vocabulary and sentence structures for making requests.

1. Hand out three blank cards to each student. Write on the board:

> *Write a situation on each card, including:*
>
> - *a reason (i.e., illness or other physical problem, last minute changes, money problems)*
> - *a request*
>
> *card a) ask for assistance with tasks at home, school/work, or a social event*
>
> *card b) change the date or time of plans*
>
> *card c) ask a favor of a non-present third person*

While students are writing on the cards, write the following dialogue format on the board:

> **Signer A:** *give reason, make request*
>
>   **B:** *decline, explain why, suggest another time/solution*
>
> **A and B:** *negotiate until you agree on the best time/solution*

When students are done writing the request cards, collect them and stack them on the table. Point to the dialogue format, then role play both Signers A and B.

For example:

> **A:** [MY] DAUGHTER SCHOOL TELEPHONE ME, TELL-TO-*me* DAUGHTER SICK, fs-RASH DCL:5*"all over body"*, SCRATCHING++. ME THINK
> BETTER GO-AWAY HOME (2h)LOOK-AT++. $\overline{\text{NOT-MIND US-TWO EAT}}$
> $\overline{\hspace{3cm}\text{q}\hspace{3cm}}$
> POSTPONE TOMORROW.
> $\overline{\hspace{2cm}\text{grimace}\hspace{2cm}}$ $\overline{\hspace{0.5cm}\text{t/q}\hspace{0.5cm}}$ $\overline{\hspace{0.5cm}\text{neg}\hspace{0.5cm}}$
> **B:** REAL/TRUE++, "wow". TOMORROW, ME CAN'T. STUCK WORK.
> $\overline{\hspace{1.5cm}\text{nod}\hspace{1.5cm}}$ $\overline{\hspace{0.5cm}\text{q}\hspace{0.5cm}}$
> FUTURE THURSDAY BETTER, "well".
> $\overline{\hspace{0.7cm}\text{q}\hspace{0.7cm}}$
> **A:** THURSDAY. FINE++.

Introduce other phrases for "declining":

ME STUCK, NONE (object, time, etc.).

<u>   q</u>   <u>neg</u>   <u>nod</u>   <u>q</u>
!NOW!, CAN'T, MUST (do other thing), CAN LATER, TIME+(#), "well".

                 <u>neg</u>
"wave-no" BETTER NOT ME, BETTER SELF++ (task).

2. Call two students up front, and have one of them pick a card from the stack and sign the request to the other student. Make sure students signing for A use one of the following sentence structures:

request help with tasks

(give reason),	<u> </u> NOT-MIND	GO-TO HELP	<u> q </u> (task) ICL"*task with tool/utensil*" PICK-UP (person/thing) GET (object) (object) BRING-TO (place) WASH"*object*" etc.

request time change

(explain situation),	<u> </u> NOT-MIND CAN	MEETING APPOINTMENT EAT PARTY BASEBALL etc.	POSTPONE PREPONE	<u> q </u> [TIME+#] [TOMORROW] [FUTURE+MONTH]

make indirect request

<u> </u> NOT-MIND YOU	ASK-TO-*person* TELL-TO-*person* INFORM-*person* SUMMON-*person*	(name)	<u> q </u> (object) GIVE-TO-*me* CALL-BY-PHONE-*me* TELL-TO-*me* INFORM-*me* SHOW-TO-*me* COME-TO SEE ME

Repeat procedure with other students. Then divide the class into pairs and distribute a card to each pair. Circulate the cards after each pair has practiced a situation.

BREAKAWAY

NUMBERS
Practice clock numbers
Bring airline flight schedules or other timetables to class. Have students practice asking and telling arrival and departure times (see Level 1, Unit 12, p. 277 for review).

SIGN PRODUCTION

"Asking Permission"

Purpose: To practice vocabulary and sentence structures for asking permission, as well as different possible responses (agree, decline and hedge).

1. Write the following dialogue format on the board:

Signer A: *ask permission*
     B: *ask for clarification* *
     A: *clarify*
     B: *respond:*
          (1) agree, with condition   *(4) decline, suggest other solution*
          (2) agree, tell shortcomings   *(5) hedge*
          (3) decline, tell why
     A: *respond*

2. Show the "Asking Permission" transparency (see Materials Appendix, p. 69). Role play the Sample Situation. Introduce vocabulary as appropriate, using the sentence structure below:

ask for permission

[[give reason]],	NOT-MIND ME BORROW PERMIT** ME USE	$\overline{\qquad}^{q}$ (money or object)
	NOT-MIND ALL-RIGHT ME CAN ME #OK PERMIT	$\overline{\qquad}^{q}$ (2h)SCL:V*"two people trade places"* TAKE-FROM*"place"* (object) (object) MOVE-TO*"place"* (LCL, ICL, and other vocabulary indicating changes in environment)

---

*__***NOTE:___ The lines of dialogue within brackets are optional, and should be used when clarification is necessary.

**__*NOTE:__ The phrase $\overline{\text{PERMIT}}^{q}$ is used for asking permission in a public place (i.e., work or school), and for asking about cultural or institution-specific rules. The phrase $\overline{\text{\#OK}}^{q}$ is used in private places, i.e., someone's home or car.

Sample dialogue:

                 _____ t _____ neg _____

A: MY LAWNMOWER NOT+WORK, REFUSE START, NOT-MIND ME

                            q

BORROW YOUR++.

        q

B: NOW.

          _____ neg _____ neg

A: NO-MATTER. TODAY, TOMORROW, NO-MATTER.

                          _____ t _____ nod

B: (agree, with condition) TODAY, ME PLAN USE. TOMORROW #OK.

        nod

A: FINE, THANK-YOU.

Role play the same situation and introduce different phrases for agreeing to, declining, or hedging requests, i.e.:

    B: (agree, tell shortcomings) FINE++, BUT INFORM-*you* IX NONE fs-BAG.

                           _____ when

        YOU MOW FINISH, MUST RAKE.

    B: (decline, tell why) SORRY, SOMEONE FINISH *person*-BORROW-FROM-*me*.

                                       neg

        NOT-KNOW #WHEN #BACK-*me* NOT-KNOW.

    B: (decline, suggest other solution) SAME-AS MINE BROKE. ME BORROW-
               FROM-*person* IX-loc*"another neighbor"*. IX HAPPY *person*-LEND-TO-
               you. WHY+NOT *you*-ASK-TO-*person*.

                                            neg

    B: (hedge) "well" MY LAWNMOWER OLD. NOT GOOD ICL*"blade cutting grass"*.

                _____ stress

        !HARD! MOW.

3. Have two students come up and practice the same dialogue. Then have Signer A sit down while Signer B becomes A. Call up another student to role play B, using response (2) on the dialogue format on the board.

    Afterwards, have that Signer B become A, and call up another student to be B, using response (3) on the board. Continue this procedure until students have practiced each response on the board.

4. Divide the class into groups of six and hand out Role Play Cards to each student in a group (see Materials Appendix, pp. 70–72). Have students follow the cues on their cards, and practice dialogues based on the situations on the "Asking Permission" transparency.

NARRATIVE PRACTICE

"One Fine Day"

Purpose: To practice role shifting using inflecting verb signs to mark subject and object. Also to rehearse request vocabulary and practice simple conditional sentences.

1. Tell the story *One Fine Day** according to the outline below.

Beginning

A thirsty fox drinks the milk from a woman's pail and the woman, in anger, cuts off the fox's tail. The fox pleads with the woman to return his tail, but she demands her milk back. The fox has to ask favors from various characters in order to get his tail back:

Requests	Conditions
Fox sees cow, asks for milk	first get grass for cow, then will give milk
Fox goes to field, asks for grass	first get water for the field, then will give some grass
Fox goes to stream, asks for water	first get jug for the stream, then will give water
Fox sees young woman, asks for jug	first get blue bead for young woman, then will give jug
Fox sees peddler, asks for blue bead	first get an egg for the peddler, then will give blue bead
Fox sees hen, asks for egg	first get some grain for the hen, then will give egg

Ending

Finally, the fox goes to the miller who feels sorry for the fox and gives him some grain. The fox then gives the grain to the hen, who in turn gives an egg to the fox. Then the fox gives the egg to the peddler, who gives the fox the blue bead he requested. The fox sees the young woman and gives her the blue bead... (and so on backwards through the list above until the woman returns the fox's tail).

---

*Nonny Hogrogian, *One Fine Day*, The Macmillan Co., New York, 1971.

Sample narrative:

Beginning

ONE-DAY, FOX <*rs:fox* WALK-*cont*, THIRSTY, SEE DCL*"pail"* MILK DCL*"full pail"*> MILK, POSS WOMAN IX-loc LOOK-FOR++ WOOD+DCL*"sticks"*. FOX <*rs:fox* ICL*"hold pail and drink from it"*>, DCL*"milk all gone"*. WOMAN SCL:1*"come along"* <*rs:woman* SEE, !MAD! ICL*"grab tail"* fs-TAIL, ICL*"cut tail off"*>.

FOX <*rs:fox* BCL*"pained, rubbing hips"*, "hey" ME WANT fs-TAIL, PLEASE *you*-GIVE-TO-*me*>.

                                                 cond

WOMAN <*rs:woman* "hmm" <u>FIRST-*thumb*++, *you*-GIVE-TO-*me* MILK,</u>
                           nod
<u>*me*-GIVE-TO-*you* fs-TAIL</u>>.

Requests and Conditions

FOX <*rs:fox* #OK, WALK-*cont*, LOOK-FOR-*cont*, SEE COW, MEET, "hey"
                    neg   q
<u>ME NONE fs-TAIL.</u> NOT-MIND <u>*you*-GIVE-TO-*me* MILK,</u> *me*-GIVE-TO-*right* WOMAN, WOMAN *right*-GIVE-TO-*me* MY fs-TAIL, ME HAPPY, "well">.

                                     cond

COW <*rs:cow* "hmm" <u>FIRST-*thumb*++, *you*-GIVE-TO-*me* GRASS, *me*-GIVE-TO-*you*</u>
   nod
<u>MILK</u>>.

FOX <*rs:fox* #OK, WALK-*cont*, LOOK-FOR-*cont*, SEE GRASS+"area", MEET, "hey"
                    neg   q
<u>ME NONE fs-TAIL.</u> NOT-MIND <u>*you*-GIVE-TO-*me* GRASS,</u> *me*-GIVE-TO-*left* COW, COW *left*-GIVE-TO-*me* MILK, *me*-GIVE-TO-*right* WOMAN, WOMAN *right*-GIVE-TO-*me* MY fs-TAIL, ME HAPPY, "well">.

                                     cond

GRASS+"area" <*rs:field* "hmm" <u>FIRST-*thumb*++, *you*-GIVE-TO-*me* WATER, *me*-</u>
                   nod
<u>GIVE-TO-*you* GRASS</u>> . . .

(Continue the story adding similar dialogues according to which character the fox approached.)

Ending

FOX <*rs:fox* #OK, WALK-*cont*, LOOK-FOR-*cont*, SEE FARM+ER,
                                   neg   q
MEET, "hey" <u>ME NONE fs-TAIL.</u> NOT-MIND <u>*you*-GIVE-TO-*me* BREAD,</u>
me-GIVE-TO-*left* HEN, HEN *left*-GIVE-TO-*me* EGG,
me-GIVE-TO-*right* MAN SELLING, MAN *right*-GIVE-TO-*me* BLUE DCL*"bead"*,
me-GIVE-TO-*left* GIRL, GIRL *left*-GIVE-TO-*me* DCL*"jug"*,
me-GIVE-TO-*right* WATER+ECL*"flowing"*, ICL*"fetch water with jug"*,
ICL*"pour water on grass on left"* GRASS+"area", *left*-GIVE-TO-*me* GRASS,
me-GIVE-TO-*right* COW, COW *right*-GIVE-TO-*me* MILK,
me-GIVE-TO-*left* WOMAN, WOMAN *left*-GIVE-TO-*me* MY fs-TAIL, ME HAPPY, "well">.

FIRST-*thumb*

FARM+ER <*rs:miller* "hmm" TOUCH-HEART, PITY-*you* FOX, DCL*"small bag"* BREAD, *me*-GIVE-TO-*you*>.

FOX <*rs:fox* ICL*"get bag"* EXCITED, RUN-TO-*right*, *me*-GIVE-TO-*hen*>, HEN <*rs:hen* EAT, FINISH, LAY-EGG, GIVE-TO-*fox*>.

FOX <*rs:fox* THANK-YOU. RUN-TO-*peddler* MAN SELLING, GIVE-TO-*him*. BLUE DCL*"bead"* *he*-GIVE-TO-*me*.

RUN-TO-*girl* GIRL, GIVE-TO-*her* BLUE DCL*"bead"*>. GIRL <*rs:girl* THANK-YOU, SEW-ON, FINISH, DCL*"jug"* GIVE-TO-*fox*>.

FOX <*rs:fox* RUN-TO-*stream*, ICL*"fetch water"*, GO-TO-*field* GRASS+*"area"* ICL*"pour water on grass"*>. GRASS DCL*"grow taller"*, FOX <*rs:fox* ICL*"cut grass"*, ICL*"carry grass to cow"*>.

COW <*rs:cow* BPCL*"eat from hand"*, #OK MILK GIVE-TO-*fox*>. FOX <*rs:fox* THANK-YOU++, ICL*"hold pail of milk, give it to woman"* WOMAN>.

WOMAN <*rs:woman* #OK, fs-TAIL GIVE-TO-*fox*>. FOX <*rs:fox* RELIEVED, HAPPY>. NEVER AGAIN STEAL MILK.

Be sure to use verb signs appropriately (i.e., using inflections on verbs to indicate the subject and object) as you assume the role of the fox making the request.

2. After you have told the whole story, hand out copies of the "One Fine Day" Summary and re-tell the beginning of the story yourself (see Materials Appendix, p. 73). When you assume the role of the fox as he pleads for his tail back, call on students to finish the sentence. Students may refer to the Summary to know how to respond as the different characters. For example:

            <u>   whq</u>

T: FOX SAY "what".

                 <u>   whq</u>

S1: FOX <*rs:fox* "hey" PLEASE GIVE-TO-*me* fs-TAIL>.

                 <u>   whq</u>

T: WOMAN SAY "what".

                                                  <u>   cond</u>

S2: WOMAN <*rs:woman* "hmm" FIRST-*thumb*++, *you*-GIVE-TO-*me* MILK,

                          <u>   nod</u>

me-GIVE-TO-*you* fs-TAIL>.

Be sure students follow the structures below for their answers.

explain reason for request

> _____ neg _____ q
> FOX <*rs:fox* "hey" ME NONE fs-TAIL. NOT-MIND *you*-GIVE-TO-*me* (object),
> *me*-GIVE-TO-(*second person*) (person), (*second person*)-GIVE-TO-*me* (another
> object), *me*-GIVE-TO-(*third person*) (person), (*third person*)-GIVE-TO-*me*
> (object)>.

conditional sentence

> _____ cond*
> (person) <*rs:person* "hmm" FIRST-*thumb*++, *you*-GIVE-TO-*me* (object),
> _____ nod
> *me*-GIVE-TO-*you* (requested object)>.

Continue the same procedure as you call on other students to role play the different characters.

3. Have all students practice telling the whole story by themselves.

   Then, call on one student to begin the story, and at an appropriate time, stop him/her. Tell another student to take over and continue the story, again stopping that student at an appropriate time. Call on a third student to continue the story, etc.

   Repeat the story if needed, till at least most of the students have had a chance to participate in telling parts of the story.

STUDENT VIDEOTEXT AND WORKBOOK

1. Make sure students complete the video-interactive and other activities for this unit, either in class or for homework. Also assign the Culture/Language Notes for this unit.

End of Unit 14

---

* **NOTE:** Conditional sentences have two parts. The first part includes conditional non-manual markers: squint eyes, raise eyebrows, tilt head sideways slightly. The last part can be a question or a statement.

APPENDIX

AT THE GARAGE

1. Write out the following car problems on cards or slips of paper:

   - your turn signals won't work
   - your car won't start
   - you can't shift into first or reverse gear
   - when you drive over 50 mph your car shakes terribly
   - when you stop at a light or stop sign, your engine dies
   - when your car warms up, the alternator light goes on
   - you have a leak somewhere; when it rains, it floods behind the driver's seat
   - going up a mountain road, your car overheated; steam was pouring out
   - you have a flat tire; you also want them to rotate the tires when they put on the spare
   - your brakes don't stop the car fast enough
   - one headlight is burned out
   - when you drive at night, your headlights get increasingly dim
   - your horn doesn't work
   - your sunroof leaks
   - your high beam lights don't work
   - you need an oil change
   - your heater doesn't work; it just blows cold air
   - your windshield wipers won't turn off
   - you can't roll your window up — it's stuck
   - you locked your keys in the car

2. Distribute the cards, then call two students up front. Tell one student to role play a traveler in a foreign country where s/he doesn't know the language; tell the other student to role play a mechanic.

   The traveler must describe his/her car problem *without using signs*, but rather by acting it out or gesturing. S/he must continue until the mechanic, again without using signs, demonstrates that s/he understands the request. (Students may use descriptive, instrument, or element classifiers that could be understood without knowing ASL.)

3. After each role play, introduce the vocabulary for the car problem described. If there is no particular sign, teach students how to describe the problem with signs or more appropriate classifiers. Then have the mechanic role play the traveler, explaining the car problem on his/her card. Continue until all students have played both roles.

FAST FORWARD

1. Have the class stand in a circle. Go around the room asking each student to tell you his/her favorite sign. Then have them change the sign in the following ways:

- sign it as big as you can
- sign it as fast as you can
- sign it as slow as you can
- sign it as low as you can
- sign it as high as you can
- sign it as small as you can
- repeat it as many times as you can
- sign it backwards

- sign it as privately as you can
- sign it as cheerfully as you can
- sign it as sadly as you can
- sign it as crazy as you can
- sign it as surprised as you can
- sign it as angrily as you can
- sign it as emphatically as you can
- sign it as doubtfully as you can

2. Have each student sign a simple statement with no more than four signs. Then have them change the sentence with all the modulations above.

As well, have them change the statement into a:

- yes/no question
- wh-word question
- negative statement
- sentence with topic-comment structure

FINGERSPELLING

Commonly Fingerspelled Words

1. Sign sentences that include one commonly or appropriately fingerspelled word. Have students spell the word back to you. Make sure you vary the location of the word in the sentence (i.e., not always at the end of the sentence). Use the following words:

physical	car related	housing
!fs-SICK!	fs-(brand names, i.e., TOYOTA, CHEV)	fs-GARAGE
fs-FLU	#CAR	fs-AC (air conditioning)
fs-FEVER	fs-VAN	fs-PORCH
fs-STIFF	#BUS	fs-ROOF
fs-HURT	#SW (station wagon)	fs-DOOR
fs-CUT	#TRUCK	fs-SOFA
fs-FOOT	fs-USED	fs-OWNER
fs-DRUGS	fs-AS-IS	fs-OWN
fs-NAIL	fs-MPH	fs-RENT
fs-HAIR	#OIL	fs-SALE
fs-DR	fs-BRAKE	fs-HOTEL
	fs-CLUTCH	fs-APT
	#GAS	fs-CONDO
	fs-REG (regular gas)	fs-CABIN
	fs-KEYS	fs-CITY
	fs-LOCK	fs-ST (street)
	fs-UNLOCK	fs-AVE
		fs-BLVD

65

	Recurring	Continuous		Recurring	Continuous
	repetitive	circular		repetitive possible	circular
	repetitive	repetitive		repetitive possible	circular
	repetitive	repetitive		uninflected	circular
	repetitive	hold sign, stressed		repetitive	hold sign, stressed
	repetitive	hold sign, stressed		uninflected	circular, bigger movement
	repetitive	repetitive preferred but circular possible		uninflected	circular, bigger movement

Situation 1
"Need Help with Tasks"

You are very busy at work and need some papers xeroxed. Your colleague is on the way down to the xerox machine. Ask him/her to make the copies for you.

Situation 2A
"Need to Change Date or Time of Plan"

You've been planning a ski trip with a friend this coming weekend. Your car broke down last week and the repairs were very expensive, so now you don't have the money to go. Ask your friend if you can postpone the trip till next month.

Situation 2B
"Need to Change Date or Time of Plan"

You have dinner plans with a friend for Friday night, but your parents just called to tell you they are coming Friday morning for two weeks. Ask your friend to change the date to Wednesday or Thursday night.

Situation 3
"Want to Ask Favor of Third Person"

Last month you lent your new *Thai Food* cookbook to your friend Maureen. Now you need it back because you're planning to cook a big Thai dinner. Ask your friend (who works with Maureen) to ask her to return the book.

Situation 4
"Want to Join a Group"

You go into a restaurant and see a group of friends. After chatting with them a while, ask if you can join them at their table.

Situation 5
"Need Someone to Hold Your Place"

You are in a long checkout line at the grocery store. You just remembered you forgot to get butter. Ask the person behind you if s/he'll hold your place in line.

Sample Situation: You need to mow your lawn, but your lawnmower is not working. Your neighbor has a mower. Ask if you can borrow it.

Situation A: You need two quarters for the parking meter, but have only a twenty dollar bill with you. Approach someone you know who may have quarters.

Situation B: You need to return some books to the library, but it's pouring rain and you don't have an umbrella. Approach your roommate who has an umbrella.

Situation C: You forgot to bring five dollars to pay for gas. You don't want to be late for your morning appointment, so you approach your co-worker who may have money s/he could lend you.

Situation D: You're making cookies when you suddenly realize you don't have enough butter. Ask your neighbor if you can borrow some butter.

Situation E: You just bought a dresser and need to deliver it to your home. Ask your friend if you can borrow his/her truck for an hour.

Situation F: Your washing machine has broken down. Ask your sister who lives nearby if you can use her washer.

Situation G: At a restaurant, you sit to the right of Signer B, who is right-handed. You are left-handed. Ask to switch places. The table looks like this:

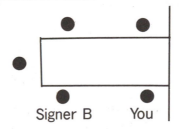

Signer B   You

Situation H: You take your kids to a pet shop. The kids want to hold the animals and pet them. Ask the shopkeeper if it's all right.

Student 1

Situation A: role play Signer A (see Situation on transparency)

Situation B: agree with condition (s/he must return the umbrella by a certain time)

Situation C: agree, tell shortcoming (you only have $3.00)

Situation D: decline, tell why (you're using all your butter now to bake a cake)

Situation E: decline, suggest other solution (your truck is broken down; give the name of another person who has a van)

Situation F: hedge (explain that your water bills are getting expensive)

Situation G: role play Signer A (see Situation on transparency)

Situation H: agree with condition (the kids can take out only one animal at a time)

Student 2

Situation A: agree with condition (that s/he give the 50 cents back tomorrow)

Situation B: agree, tell shortcoming (your umbrella won't stay open — s/he would have to hold it open)

Situation C: decline, tell why (Signer A owes you money and hasn't paid you back yet)

Situation D: decline, suggest other solution (you don't have enough butter; tell him/her to ask another neighbor)

Situation E: hedge (your truck has a flat tire)

Situation F: role play Signer A (see Situation on transparency)

Situation G: agree with condition (ask to switch chairs as well — your chair is cushioned, while Signer A's is all wood)

Situation H: agree, tell shortcoming (you have no key to open the cages; the kids will have to pet the animals through the bars)

Student 3

Situation A: agree, tell shortcoming (you only have 25 cents)

Situation B: decline, tell why (you have to go to work now, and need the umbrella)

Situation C: decline, suggest other solution (the gas station on the corner accepts any credit card or bank card)

Situation D: hedge (your butter is mixed with oil for easy spreading)

Situation E: role play Signer A (see Situation on transparency)

Situation F: agree with condition (ask your sibling to wash your clothes for you as well)

Situation G: agree, tell shortcoming (your seat is in a drafty spot)

Situation H: decline, tell why (the animals are young and can easily become sick if handled)

Student 4

Situation A: decline, tell why (you need the money for the bus)

Situation B: decline, suggest other solution (you need the umbrella, but offer your raincoat with a hood)

Situation C: hedge (you don't have cash with you now — you'd need to go to the bank which is five blocks away)

Situation D: role play Signer A (see Situation on transparency)

Situation E: agree with condition (Signer A must fill the tank)

Situation F: agree, tell shortcoming (your hot water runs out after one or two loads)

Situation G: decline, tell why (you have to leave early, so want to sit where you are, near the door)

Situation H: decline, suggest other solution (only customers interested in buying an animal can hold or pet it)

Student 5

Situation A: decline, suggest other solution (you don't have any money — suggest the name of another person Signer A can ask)

Situation B: hedge (it's not your umbrella — it belongs to someone else)

Situation C: role play Signer A (see Situation on transparency)

Situation D: agree with condition (you need the butter replaced by tonight)

Situation E: agree, tell shortcoming (your truck is filthy and covered with grease)

Situation F: decline, tell why (your machine isn't working properly)

Situation G: decline, suggest other solution (tell Signer A to ask someone else to switch)

Situation H: hedge (explain that the boss will be back soon; Signer A can ask her)

Student 6

Situation A: hedge (your spouse has your wallet, and will be back in about half an hour)

Situation B: role play Signer A (see Situation on transparency)

Situation C: agree with condition (you need the five dollars back before noon so you can have lunch)

Situation D: agree, tell shortcoming (you don't have real butter)

Situation E: decline, tell why (your friend has borrowed your truck for ten days)

Situation F: decline, suggest other solution (your sibling could drop off the dirty laundry, and you'll wash it later in the day)

Situation G: hedge (explain that it doesn't bother you at all)

Situation H: role play Signer A (see Situation on transparency)

"ONE FINE DAY"
(for p. 62)
Summary

Beginning

A thirsty fox drinks the milk from a woman's pail and the woman, in anger, cuts off the fox's tail. The fox pleads with the woman to return his tail, but she demands her milk back. The fox has to ask favors from various characters in order to get his tail back:

Requests	Conditions
Fox sees cow, asks for milk	first get grass for cow, then will give milk
Fox goes to field, asks for grass	first get water for the field, then will give some grass
Fox goes to stream, asks for water	first get jug for the stream, then will give water
Fox sees young woman, asks for jug	first get blue bead for young woman, then will give jug
Fox sees peddler, asks for blue bead	first get an egg for the peddler, then will give blue bead
Fox sees hen, asks for egg	first get some grain for the hen, then will give egg

Ending

Finally, the fox goes to the miller who feels sorry for the fox and gives him some grain. The fox then gives the grain to the hen, who in turn gives an egg to the fox. Then the fox gives the egg to the peddler, who gives the fox the blue bead he requested. The fox sees the young woman and gives her the blue bead . . . (and so on backwards through the list above until the woman returns the fox's tail).

UNIT 15

EXCHANGING PERSONAL INFORMATION: LIFE EVENTS
O V E R V I E W

DIALOGUE FORMAT:

Signer A: ask about nationality
        B: respond, narrate
            family history

SAMPLE DIALOGUE:

                              _____t_____   _____q_____
Signer A: YOUR WIFE fs-VERA 100 PERCENT SPAIN.
        B: "wave-no", IX CONFLICT MANY, FRANCE, ITALY,

                                                    _____t_____
fs-PORTUGUESE, AMERICAN-INDIAN. POSS MOTHER,
                       _____t_____   _____t_____
POSS*"mom"* FATHER FROM ITALY. MOTHER FROM

                                    _____t_____
FRANCE. FATHER, POSS*"dad"* FATHER MOVE-TO*"here"*
FROM fs-PORTUGAL, FALL-IN-LOVE AMERICAN-
INDIAN WOMAN, THAT-ONE fs-VERA GRANDMOTHER,
MARRIED, BORN fs-VERA'S FATHER. IX*"Vera"*

                                   _____nod_____
fs-VERA CONFLICT++ !MANY! INTERESTING.

VOCABULARY:

life events	life events	nationality signs	numbers
BE-RAISED	DIED	GENERATION	numbers: 110–119
GO-UP-YEARS	LAID-OFF	FULL	dates and addresses
GRADUATE	BURN-DOWN	HALF	
FALL-IN-LOVE	DROP-OUT	(2h)alt.HALF	other
CONCEIVE	TAKE-UP TEST	CONFLICT	FROM
MOVE-TO	PASS	STRONG	ITSELF
OFFER	LICENSE	100 PERCENT	HAPPEN
PROMOTE	ESCAPE	COUNTRY	WRONG
TRANSFER	MESS-UP		THEREABOUTS
PRINCIPAL	SOLDIER	time signs	LIE++ (Breakaway)
CAR-ACCIDENT	SUMMON	UP-TILL-NOW	FICTIONAL (Breakaway)
RETIRED	KILL++	LATER-ON	countries and continents
SETTLE-DOWN	WAR	BEFORE-EVENT	vocabulary for why people migrate

SENTENCE STRUCTURES:

tell about life events using when clause (age)

	when	
_____		
ME	(age)	(event)

tell about life events using when clause (event)

	when		
_____		[LATER-ON]	
ME	(event)	[(time sign)]	(event)

tell about an unexpected change in events

(event)	(time)	WRONG	(change or result)

ask nationality of name

<u> t </u> NAME fs-(name),	ITSELF POSS*"country"*	<u> q </u> (country) [NAME]
NAME fs-(name),	ITSELF	<u> whq </u> FROM WHERE
	<u> whq </u> #WHAT COUNTRY "what"	

ask if full-blooded

<u> </u> YOU (person)	FULL 100 PERCENT GENERATION FROM	<u> q </u> (country)

confirm

YES	FULL STRONG	(country)

correct and elaborate

#NO "wave-no"	ME	HALF (country), HALF (country) CONFLICT++ [MANY] (list countries) LITTLE-BIT (country), STRONG (another country) MY FATHER (country), MY MOTHER (country)

GRAMMAR:

when clauses
phrasing for sequencing events
contrastive structure
possessive forms: POSS, 'S
descriptive and locative
   classifiers (Breakaway)

SIGN ILLUSTRATIONS:

BE-RAISED (see p. 76)
GO-UP-YEARS (see p. 76)
LATER-ON (see p. 76)
BEFORE-EVENT (see p. 84)
GENERATION (see p. 88)
FICTIONAL (see p. 104)

MATERIALS:

"Life Events" transparency
"The Family" transparency
"Dates and Addresses" worksheet
"Immigration and Family History"
  transparency

children's wooden blocks (Breakaway)
map of the world

INTRODUCTION

Telling About Life Events

1. Show the "Life Events" transparency (see Materials Appendix, p. 105). Write in the name Jose and use the following narrative to introduce when clauses:*

BE-RAISED

GO-UP-YEARS

LATER-ON

> **T:** fs-JOSE BORN 1920.
>
>   <u>when</u>
> OLD+5, ENTER DEAF-SCHOOL IX-loc ARIZONA. BE-RAISED, GRADUATE 1937.
>
>   <u>when</u>
> ENTER GALLAUDET, GO-UP-YEARS. GRADUATE, TRANSFER fs-IOWA DEAF-SCHOOL, TEACH++.
>
> LATER-ON MEET WIFE, FALL-IN-LOVE, GO-STEADY 4+YEAR. MARRIED 1947.
> <u>when</u>
> 1949, BUY HOUSE. 2+YEAR LATER-ON, SON BORN.
>
> fs-MINN DEAF-SCHOOL OFFER-*him* WORK, PRINCIPAL. SELL HOUSE, MOVE-AWAY fs-MINN 1953. LATER-ON WIFE CONCEIVE, BE-PREGNANT, BORN GIRL.
>
> LATER-ON !WRONG! WIFE CAR-ACCIDENT, !#KILLED!.
>
> fs-JOSE ALONE-*cont* 5+YEAR.
>
>   <u>when</u>
> BOY*"left"* OLD+9, GIRL*"right"* OLD+5, [fs-JOSE] MARRIED AGAIN, SECOND WIFE.
>
>   <u>when</u>
> OLD+60, RETIRED. LATER-ON 1 YEAR MOVE-AWAY fs-FLA. SETTLE-DOWN.

2. Review the vocabulary and phrases in the story by asking students questions about Jose's life. Use the following when-clause sentence structures to ask the questions:

ask when by age

<u>when</u> fs-JOSE OLD+(#),	whq "what" HAPPEN (2h)#DO++

*****NOTE:** The non-manual markers for when clauses are similar to topicalization and conditionals, including eyebrow raise and slight head tilt. Semantically, when clauses mean "at that time," or "when that time/event occurred." When clauses, like conditionals, occur at the beginning of the sentence.

Sample sentences:

       <u>   when   </u>   <u> whq </u>
fs-JOSE OLD+17, (2h)#DO++.   (graduated from the school for the deaf)

       <u>   when   </u>   <u> whq </u>
fs-JOSE OLD+33, "what" HAPPEN.   (got job as principal at Minnesota School for the Deaf)

ask when by year

<u>when</u> (year),	fs-JOSE (2h)#DO++ <u> whq </u> <u> whq </u> "what" HAPPEN

Sample sentences:

<u>when</u>   <u> whq </u>
1949, "what" HAPPEN.   (bought house)

<u>when</u>   <u> whq </u>
1960, fs-JOSE (2h)#DO++.   (remarried)

ask when in relation to another event

<u>when</u> (event),	[LATER-ON] [(length of time)]	<u> whq </u> "what" HAPPEN

Sample sentences:

                      <u> when </u>   <u> whq </u>
fs-JOSE, WIFE THEY-TWO GO-STEADY 4+YEAR, "what" HAPPEN. (they got married)

       <u> when </u>   <u> whq </u>
fs-JOSE BORN GIRL, LATER-ON "what" HAPPEN. (wife was killed in car accident)

3. Begin the narrative again, this time having students take turns signing the next event in Jose's life. Check that students sign when clauses correctly.

SIGN PRODUCTION

"Tell About Life Events: Using When Clauses"

Purpose: To practice non-manual markers for when clauses (eyebrow raise, head tilt), referring to age and event.

By Age

1. Write on the board:

> *Tell about life events*
>
> * *by referring to age*

Show the "Life Events" transparency again. Point to the second picture (Jose entering the school for the deaf), and sign:

          <u>when</u>
T: fs-JOSE OLD+5, ENTER DEAF-SCHOOL IX-loc ARIZONA.

S: (copy sentence)

                  <u>when</u>
T: (point to the third picture and sign) fs-JOSE OLD+17, GRADUATE.

S: (copy sentence)

T: (point to the picture of Jose at age 22, and have students sign the sentence using age and when clause)

          <u>when</u>
S: fs-JOSE OLD+22, GRADUATE, TRANSFER fs-IOWA DEAF-SCHOOL.

T: (point to the picture of Jose at age 33)

          <u>when</u>
S: fs-JOSE OLD+33, OFFER-*him* #JOB, PRINCIPAL.

T: (point to the picture of Jose at age 40)

          <u>when</u>
S: fs-JOSE OLD+40, MARRIED AGAIN.

T: (point to the picture of Jose at age 60)

          <u>when</u>
S: fs-JOSE OLD+60, RETIRED.

2. Continue practicing when clauses by having students talk about their own life events. They should use the following sentence structure:

tell about life events using when clause (age)

_____ when	
ME (age)	(event)

First sign an example, i.e.:

_____ when
T: ME OLD+5, MY SISTER BORN.

Call on students to sign similar sentences, filling in their own life events, i.e.:

_____ when
S: ME OLD+5, (student fills in with own life event)

_____ when
ME OLD+16, (student fills in with own life event)

_____ when
ME OLD+25, (student fills in with own life event)

etc.

Check that students use appropriate non-manual markers for when clauses.

3. Vary the activity by talking about others. Begin by signing:

_____ when
T: MY MOTHER OLD+50, BECOME GRANDMOTHER.

Have students continue with similar sentences about other people in their lives, i.e.:

cousin	brother	aunt	daughter
father	wife	uncle	son
sister	husband		

By Event

4. Add to the board:

Tell about life events

- *by referring to age*
- *by referring to other events*

Show the "Life Events" transparency again and point to the picture of Jose graduating from Gallaudet. Then sign:

_____ when
T: fs-JOSE GRADUATE GALLAUDET, TRANSFER fs-IOWA DEAF-SCHOOL.

S: (copy sentence)

T: (point to the picture of Jose and his girlfriend going steady, then point to the picture of their wedding)
_____ when
fs-JOSE FALL-IN-LOVE, GO-STEADY, 4+YEAR MARRIED.

S: (copy sentence)

T: (point to the picture of Jose and his wife buying a house, then to the picture of their son being born)
_____ when
THEY-TWO BUY HOUSE, LATER-ON SON BORN.

Continue pointing to other pictures, and sign sentences like the following:

_____ when
DAUGHTER BORN, LATER-ON WIFE #KILLED.
_____ when
RETIRED, 1+YEAR MOVE-AWAY fs-FLA.

etc.

5. Have students talk about their own life events. They should use the following sentence structure:

tell about life events using when clause (event)

_____ when		
ME (event)	[LATER-ON] [(time sign)]	(event)

First sign an example, then call on students to sign similar sentences, filling in their own life events, i.e.:

---

                  when

T: ME MARRIED, LATER-ON CONCEIVE. BORN GIRL.

                  when

S: ME MARRIED, LATER-ON (student fills in with own life event)

                  when

T: ME GRADUATE, TWO-MONTHS GET WORK.

                  when

S: ME GRADUATE, TWO-MONTHS (student fills in with own life event)

Call on other students to talk about their lives by referring to different events. First give them cues and have them complete the sentences, i.e.:

                  when

ME MOVE-TO CALIFORNIA, 1+YEAR LATER-ON (student fills in with own life event)

                  when

ME GET WORK, ONE-WEEK LATER-ON (student fills in with own life event)

etc.

Check that students use appropriate non-manual behaviors for when clauses.

6. Vary the activity by talking about others. Begin by signing:

---

                  when

T: HUSBAND GET #JOB, 2+YEAR LATER-ON PROMOTE.

Have students continue with similar sentences about other people in their lives, i.e.:

boss	neighbor	teacher	boyfriend
co-worker	friend	student	girlfriend

"Telling About Life Events Without When Clause"

Purpose: To practice other ways of telling about life events: by telling the year an event occurred, by sequencing events, by telling about unexpected changes.

By Year

1. Add the following to the board:

> *Tell about life events*
>
> > • *by referring to age*
> > • *by referring to other events*
> > • ***by year***

Show the "Life Events" transparency again and point to the very first picture (Jose's birth). Then sign:

> **T:** fs-JOSE BORN 1920.
>
> **S:** (copy sentence)
>
> **T:** (point to the third picture, Jose's high school graduation, and sign)
>
>   fs-JOSE GRADUATE 1937.
>
> **S:** (copy sentence)

Continue pointing to other pictures and have students sign sentences like the following:

S: IX*"Jose"* GRADUATE GALLAUDET 1942.

   IX*"Jose"* START TEACHING 1942.

   IX*"Jose"* SON BORN 1951.

   IX*"Jose"* MOVE-TO fs-MINN 1953.

   IX*"Jose"* WIFE DIED 1955.

2. Have students talk about their own life events using the following sentence structure:

tell about life events by year (no when clause)

(person)	(event)	(year)

First sign an example, i.e.:

> **T:** ME BORN 1947.
>
> 　ME GRADUATE 1966.
>
> 　ME MARRIED 1969.
>
> 　ME DIVORCED 1978.

Call on students to sign similar sentences, talking about their own life events.

Sequence of Events

3. Add the following to the board:

> *Tell about life events*
>
> - *by referring to age*
> - *by referring to other events*
> - *by year*
> - ***by sequencing events***

Show the "Life Events" transparency again and point to the second and third pictures (at the school for the deaf). Then sign:

> **T:** fs-JOSE ENTER DEAF-SCHOOL, BE-RAISED, GRADUATE.
>
> **S:** (copy sentence)
>
> **T:** (point to the fourth and fifth pictures, at Gallaudet, and sign)
>
> 　IX*"Jose"* ENTER GALLAUDET, GO-UP-YEARS, GRADUATE.
>
> **S:** (copy sentence)
>
> **T:** (point to pictures seven, eight and nine)
>
> **S:** IX*"Jose"* MEET, FALL-IN-LOVE, GO-STEADY, MARRIED.
>
> **T:** (point to the pictures of Jose getting a job and moving to Minnesota)
>
> **S:** fs-JOSE OFFER-*him* #JOB, SELL HOUSE, MOVE-AWAY fs-MINN.

4. Have students talk about their own life events using the following sentence structure:

tell the sequence of events

(event)	(event)	(event)

Use a head tilt (which functions like a comma) between telling two events. To do this, tilt your head backwards slightly for a short time. The head tilt represents a shift to the next time frame, in chronological order. See Student Videotext (Unit 15) for examples.

First sign an example, i.e.:

ME GRADUATE COLLEGE, TRAVEL*"around"*, #BACK ARRIVE, START WORK.

Then call on students to sign similar sentences about their own life events.

Variation: Ask students to give you a sequence of events that lead up to a particular event. For example, ask what people have to do to get a driver's license:

BEFORE-EVENT

	when		cs	whq
T:	GET CAR LICENSE,	BEFORE-EVENT	(2h)#DO++.	
S:	GET PERMIT, PRACTICE DRIVING, TAKE-UP TEST, PASS.			

Continue asking about other events, and have students sign their own sentences using the structure above, i.e.:

- getting a new car
- getting a dog
- moving out of your parents' home

- traveling overseas
- getting a divorce
- getting a job

By Unexpected Changes in Events

5. Add to the board:

> *Tell about life events*
>
> - *by referring to age*
> - *by referring to other events*
> - *by year*
> - *by sequencing events*
> - ***by unexpected changes***

Demonstrate the use of the sign WRONG to show an unexpected change in events. Point to the fourth picture (of Jose at Gallaudet) and sign the following example:

T: ENTER COLLEGE, GO-UP-YEARS*"to sophomore"*, WRONG, !SICK!, DROP-OUT*"sophomore year"*.

S: (copy sentence)

T: (point to the seventh picture, of Jose and his girlfriend, and sign)

  FALL-IN-LOVE, GO-STEADY, WRONG, CONCEIVE.

S: (copy sentence)

Point to other pictures on the transparency and ask what unexpected events could occur. Make sure students use the following structure:

tell about an unexpected change in events

(event) (time)	WRONG	(change or result)

For example:

T: (point to the sixth picture)

S: WORK TWO-MONTHS, WRONG, LAID-OFF.

T: (point to the picture of Jose and his wife buying a house)

S: BUY HOUSE, LATER-ON, WRONG, BURN-DOWN.

Variation: Ask students what unexpected event could occur after another event. For example, ask what could happen after getting driver's license:

_____t_____whq
T: GET CAR LICENSE, TWO-WEEKS, WRONG, "what".

S: BE-LOST.

T: (then have the student sign the whole sentence)

S: GET CAR LICENSE, TWO-WEEKS, WRONG, BE-LOST.

Continue asking about other events, and have students sign their own sentences using the structure above, i.e., ask about:

- getting a new car
- getting a dog
- moving out of parents' home
- traveling overseas

NARRATIVE PRACTICE

"Personal History"

Purpose: To practice combining when clauses, sequencing events, and using the signs LATER-ON and WRONG to talk about one's life.

1. Write the following narrative sequence on the board:

> (1) *tell when and where you were born*
> (2) *tell about life events by referring to age, event,*
> *year, sequence, and unexpected changes*
> (3) *end with current situation*

Tell all students to prepare a one to two minute narrative about their lives, following the sequence on the board. Be sure they use an example of each sentence structure taught, as well as the time sign LATER-ON and the conjunction sign WRONG.

2. Then divide the class into groups and have students practice signing their narratives to each other. Encourage students to be active listeners by responding, nodding, and asking questions during the narratives.

    After each narrative, the other students in the group should make notes on the ages, years and events that were recounted.

3. Afterwards, call a few students up front to sign their narratives to the whole class.

BREAKAWAY ▬▬▬▬▬▬▬▬▬▬▬▬▬▬▬▬▬▬▬▬▬▬▬▬▬▬

BUILDING BLOCKS
(see Appendix, p. 99)

Purpose: To practice giving instructions using descriptive and locative classifiers, and to work on signer's perspective.

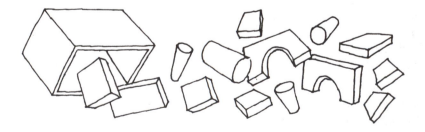

INTRODUCTION

Discussing Nationalities

1. Show a map of the world and introduce vocabulary for continents and countries:

North America

NORTH AMERICA
AMERICA
CANADA
MEXICO
fs-CUBA
fs-PR

Central and South America

CENTER/MIDDLE AMERICA
SOUTH AMERICA
names of all countries
  fingerspelled

Africa

AFRICA
EGYPT
SOUTH AFRICA
all others fingerspelled

Europe

EUROPE
FINLAND
NORWAY
SWEDEN
DENMARK
RUSSIA
HOLLAND
FRANCE
ENGLAND
IRELAND
SCOTLAND
GERMANY
SWITZERLAND
ITALY
SPAIN
GREECE
POLAND
AUSTRIA
YUGOSLAVIA
all others fingerspelled

Middle East

ISRAEL (JEWISH)
IRAN
all others fingerspelled

Far East

ASIA
JAPAN
CHINA
TAIWAN
PHILIPPINES
KOREA
INDIA*
VIETNAM
HONG-KONG
all others fingerspelled

other

AUSTRALIA
all others fingerspelled

2. Refer to different countries and ask students questions, i.e.:

- Give the name of a country and ask what countries are around its borders.

- Ask what language is spoken in different countries.

- Give the name of a famous person and ask where s/he is from, i.e.:
  — Mao (China)
  — Gandhi (India)
  — the Pope (lives in Italy)
  — Winnie Mandela (South Africa)

- Ask what country is famous for:
  — making cars (give names: Volvo, Fiat, Honda, VW)
  — making wine
  — oil
  — banking
  — vodka, beer
  — diamonds

- Ask what countries or regions originated these customs:
  — bullfighting (Spain)
  — the polka dance (Poland)
  — a couple jumping over a broom on the floor during a wedding ceremony (Africa)
  — women wearing the veil over their faces (Middle East)

---

*NOTE: Distinguish this sign from AMERICAN-INDIAN.

Family Nationality

1. Draw the following family trees on the board:

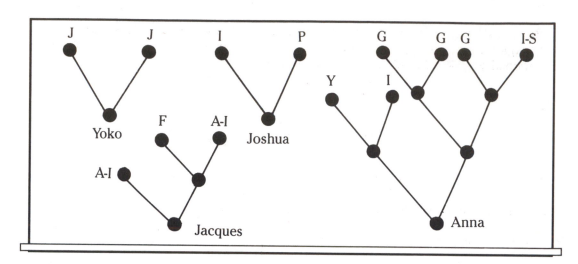

Point to the first tree and introduce the signs GENERATION and FULL:

> **T:** fs-YOKO POSS FAMILY **GENERATION FULL** JAPAN.

Introduce another phrase for "full-blooded": 100 PERCENT.

Point to the second tree and introduce the sign (2h)alt.HALF:

>   t   t
> **T:** fs-JOSHUA POSS MOTHER JEWISH, POSS FATHER POLAND, IX*"Joshua"*
> **(2h)alt.HALF**.

GENERATION

Point to the third tree and introduce the signs HALF and STRONG:

>   t   t
> **T:** fs-JACQUES POSS MOTHER AMERICAN-INDIAN, POSS FATHER **HALF**
> FRANCE, **HALF** AMERICAN-INDIAN, IX*"Jacques"* **STRONG**
> AMERICAN-INDIAN.

Point to the fourth tree and introduce the sign CONFLICT++:

>   t
> **T:** fs-ANNA POSS FATHER STRONG GERMANY, LITTLE-BIT IRELAND, SCOTLAND.
>   t
> POSS MOTHER HALF YUGOSLAVIA, HALF ITALY. IX*"Anna"*
> **CONFLICT++** MANY.

2. Then ask students their nationalities, and review the following signs as applicable:

GENERATION   FULL   HALF

STRONG   CONFLICT   (2h)alt.HALF

Be sure students use contrastive structure when talking about a mixed family background. Contrastive structure involves signing on one side for the mother's nationality and the other side for the father's.

SIGN PRODUCTION

"Ng, Isn't That Vietnamese?"

Purpose: To practice asking and telling about nationalities.

1. Write the following dialogue format on the board:

> **Signer A:** *ask B's name*
> **B:** *give full name*
> **A:** *repeat last name, ask nationality of name*
> **B:** *correct or confirm*
> **A:** *ask if B is full-blooded (nationality)*
> **B:** *confirm, or correct and explain*

Role play both Signers A and B in a dialogue like the following:

> $\overline{\text{whq}}$
> **A:** YOU NAME "what".
>
> **B:** fs-KEN-MIKOS.
>
> $\overline{\text{t}}$ $\overline{\text{q}}$
> **A:** fs-MIKOS, ITSELF GREEK NAME.
>
> $\overline{\text{neg}}$
> **B:** #NO++, POLAND NAME.
>
> $\overline{\text{q}}$
> **A:** OH-I-SEE, YOU 100 PERCENT POLAND.
>
> $\overline{\text{neg}}$
> **B:** #NO++, ME HALF POLAND, HALF fs-CZECH.

2. Call up a student to role play Signer B, while you sign for A using the following sentence structures:

ask nationality of name (line 3)

<u> t</u> NAME fs-(name),	<u> </u> ITSELF POSS *"country"*	<u> q</u> (country) [NAME]
NAME fs-(name),	ITSELF	<u> whq</u> FROM WHERE
		<u> whq</u> #WHAT COUNTRY "what"

ask if full-blooded (line 5)

<u> </u> YOU (person)	FULL 100 PERCENT GENERATION FROM	<u> q</u> (country)

Signer B should respond with either of the following sentence structures:

confirm (line 6)

YES	FULL STRONG	(country)

correct and elaborate (line 6)

#NO "wave-no"	ME	HALF (country), HALF (country) CONFLICT++ [MANY] (list countries) LITTLE-BIT (country), STRONG (another country) MY FATHER (country), MY MOTHER (country)

3. Have Signer B become Signer A and select another student to be Signer B. Have the whole class watch both signers. Continue this procedure with the rest of the class.

EXTENDED COMPREHENSION

The McCarthy Family

1. Make a transparency of the "The Family" illustration (see Materials Appendix, p. 106) and show it to the class.

   Introduce each family member by fingerspelling their names as follows:

Point to:	Introduce name:
man kissing woman (son)	Ian McCarthy
pregnant woman (daughter-in law)	Elena McCarthy, (maiden name Gomez)*
woman reading (daughter)	Suzie
young girl (granddaughter)	Kristie
grandfather	Brian McCarthy
grandmother	Betty McCarthy, (maiden name Mueller)*

2. Explain the relationships and backgrounds:

   • it's the first marriage for Elena, but the second marriage for Ian

   • Kristie is Ian's daughter from a previous marriage

   • Suzie is now divorced

   • Betty's mother is still living at the age of 92

   Then tell about the nationalities of each family member:

   > **T:** IX GRANDFATHER GENERATION FROM IRELAND.
   >
   > IX GRANDMOTHER GENERATION FROM GERMANY.
   >
   > IX fs-ELENA GENERATION FROM MEXICO. IX FULL MEXICO.
   >
   > IX fs-IAN SELF HALF IRELAND, HALF GERMANY.
   >
   > IX fs-KRISTIE FIRST-*thumb* MOTHER SWEDEN, FRANCE.
   >
   >   ‾‾‾‾t‾‾‾‾
   > IX FATHER IRELAND, GERMANY. IX*"girl"* CONFLICT++.
   >
   > IX fs-SUZIE #EX+HUSBAND ITALY. THEY-TWO NONE CHILDREN.
   >
   > IX fs-KRISTIE POSS fs-GREAT+GRANDMOTHER FULL GERMANY. STILL LIVE, OLD+92.

---

*NOTE: One way to express the concept of "maiden name" is with the phrase BEFORE-EVENT MARRY.

3. Review the relationships and nationalities of the people in the picture by asking:

- the name of each person
- how each person is related to the others in the transparency
- which family member has remarried or divorced
- how Kristie is related to her father's second wife
- nationalities of some family members:
  — Suzie's ex-husband
  — Elena
  — Kristie
- the nationality of the name McCarthy
- Elena's maiden name

John's and Vera's Family Tree

1. Sign a narrative about the family background of a fictional person named John:

> _____ q/t _____ t
>
> **T:** IX fs-JOHN, POSS MOTHER'S MOTHER+FATHER LONG-AGO BORN, BE-RAISED IX-loc POLAND, MOVE-TO AMERICA 1930.
>
> _____ t
>
> POSS FATHER'S MOTHER+FATHER, BORN IX-loc RUSSIA, MOVE-TO AMERICA THEREABOUTS 1931.
>
> _____ t
>
> MOTHER+FATHER MEET IX-loc SCHOOL, (2h)BE-RAISED, GO-STEADY, MARRIED, BORN fs-JOHN.

Have students draw John's family tree on paper (see top of p. 93).

2. Sign another narrative as follows:

> _____ t
>
> **T:** fs-VERA, GENERATION CONFLICT++ MANY, FRANCE, ITALY,
>
> _____ t
>
> fs-PORTUGUESE, AMERICAN-INDIAN. POSS MOTHER,
>
> _____ t _____ t
>
> POSS*"mom"* FATHER FROM ITALY. MOTHER FROM FRANCE.
>
> _____ t
>
> FATHER, POSS*"dad"* FATHER MOVE-TO*"here"* FROM fs-PORTUGAL, FALL-IN-LOVE AMERICAN-INDIAN WOMAN, THAT-ONE fs-VERA GRANDMOTHER, MARRIED, BORN fs-VERA'S FATHER. IX*"Vera"* fs-VERA
>
> _____ nod
>
> CONFLICT++ !MANY! INTERESTING.

Have students draw Vera's family tree (see top of p. 93).

John's family tree

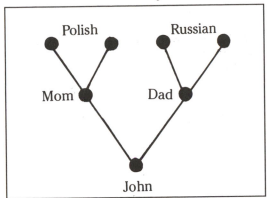

Vera's family tree

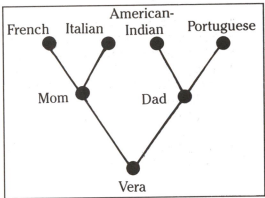

SIGN PRODUCTION

"Guess Whose Family Tree"

Purpose: To practice describing a family tree using appropriate possessive pronouns and contrastive structure.

1. Draw a diagram of a family tree on the board as follows:

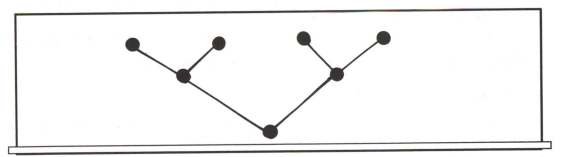

2. Hand out an index card to each student. Tell students to draw their own family trees, and to fill in the nationality for each person on the tree. Tell students *not* to write in their names.

3. Collect all the cards, shuffle them and distribute one to each student.

4. Students should now describe the family tree on the card to the whole class, using sentences like the following:

t **T:** PERSON IX*"point to card"*, POSS*"card"* MOTHER*"right"* (nationality), FATHER*"left"* (nationality).

The student whose nationality was described should then identify him/herself.

BREAKAWAY ▬▬▬▬▬▬

NUMBERS

Introduce numbers 110 – 119

Dates and Addresses
(see Appendix, p. 101)

Purpose: To practice numbers and fingerspelling for dates and addresses.

INTRODUCTION

Telling About Family History

1. Write on the board:

Why people migrate:

    economic reasons
    persecution
    war
    family reasons

Lead a discussion about why people migrate by expanding on each reason on the board. Introduce signs, phrases or descriptions for the following:

economic reasons

no jobs, no money
natural disasters (famine, epidemic, earthquake, flood, drought)
better opportunities in the other country (i.e., gold rush, free enterprise)
people forced to come as slaves or indentured servants

persecution

people not free to worship or attend church
people not allowed to express their thoughts and opinions about the government
people not allowed to choose the job they want, or to travel
people are oppressed and killed because of race, religion, or beliefs

war

people suffer during war because of food shortage, no supplies, destruction
people leave to avoid the draft/military

family reasons

divorce or marriage
better education
better medical care

2. Review by asking students about their nationalities and how their families ended up where they are, i.e.:

- nationalities on both sides of the family?
- when did family members on both sides come to this country?
- for what reasons?
- did they move from place to place within this country?

etc.

SIGN PRODUCTION

"The Immigrants"

Purpose: To practice using possessive pronouns and contrastive structure in narrating family immigration history.

1. Show the "Immigration and Family History" transparency (see Materials Appendix, p. 109). Tell students that you will role play Chris, and show possessive pronouns (both POSS and 'S) for all possible relationships by pointing to any two persons on the transparency, i.e.:

father to you (Chris):	MY FATHER
grandmother to you:	MY GRANDMOTHER
great-grandmother to you:	MY fs-GREAT GRANDMOTHER
great-grandmother to father:	MY FATHER POSS*"father"* GRANDMOTHER, (or) MY FATHER'S GRANDMOTHER
great-grandmother to grandfather:	MY GRANDFATHER, POSS*"grandfather"* MOTHER+IN-LAW, (or) MY GRANDFATHER'S MOTHER+IN-LAW

2. Write on the board:

```
Narrative sequence:

tell who
tell background
tell about changes
tell about move
```

Explain that you (as Chris) will tell about your forebears. Tell about **your great-grandparents** in a narrative like the following:

Narrative sequence:	Sample narrative:
• tell who: use POSS and/or contrastive structure	MY GRANDMOTHER, POSS MOTHER+FATHER...
• tell background	...BORN RUSSIA, RICH, FAMOUS...

when

| • tell about changes | ...WRONG, 1900 THEREABOUTS, WAR. RUSSIA HATE RICH, KILL++. MOTHER+FATHER ESCAPE, GO-TO ENGLAND. NONE WORK. FATHER HAVE COUSIN LIVE IX-loc SCOTLAND. |

when

| • tell about move | THEREABOUTS 1917, MOVE-TO [SCOTLAND]. BORN GRANDMOTHER. |

Have students imitate the narrative to develop fluency. Check their use of POSS.

3. Follow the same sequence to sign a narrative about **your grandparents**. For example:

Narrative sequence:	Sample narrative:
• tell who	REMEMBER MY GRANDMOTHER BORN

cs

SCOTLAND, THAT-ONE MY FATHER POSS MOTHER.

| • tell background | BE-RAISED SCOTLAND, FINE. |
| • tell about changes | WRONG, WORLD WAR SECOND, EUROPE MESS-UP, AMERICA SOLDIER PCL*"flock to"* [EUROPE]. GRANDMOTHER MEET GRANDFATHER, HIMSELF AMERICA. |

cs

LATER-ON MARRIED.

| • tell about move | MOVE-TO*"here"* AMERICA 1945. LIVE IX-loc NEW-YORK. BORN FATHER. |

Have students repeat the narrative after you.

4. Following the same sequence, sign a narrative about **your parents**. For example:

Narrative sequence:	Sample narrative:
• tell who	FATHER BORN 1947.

when

| • tell background | BE-RAISED NEW-YORK. OLD+15, FAMILY MOVE-TO fs-UTAH. |

* tell about changes   LATER-ON 1965 ENTER UNIVERSITY fs-OF TEXAS, GO-UP-YEARS *"to sophomore year"*. WRONG, ARMY SUMMON-*him*, GO-AWAY WAR VIETNAM.

                                      _____when_____
* tell about move   GO-TO VIETNAM, MEET MOTHER, HERSELF
                                                    ____when____
                              VIETNAM. LATER-ON, MOTHER OLD+18, MARRIED. MOVE-TO AMERICA, #BACK fs-UTAH, BORN ME 1969.

Have students repeat the narrative after you.

5. Sign a narrative about **yourself**, for example:

Narrative sequence: Sample narrative:

* tell who   ME NAME fs-CHRIS.

                                              _____when_____
* tell background   BE-RAISED fs-UTAH. OLD+4, SISTER BORN.

* tell about changes   (Invent your own narrative. Suggestions: parents divorced; parents moved; parent(s) died; you have baby out of wedlock, etc.)

* tell about move   (Invent your own narrative. Suggestions: move in with one parent; after parents' death, you live with grandparents in Utah; marry because of baby, etc.)

NARRATIVE PRACTICE

"Telling Family History"

Purpose: To review when-clause vocabulary for talking about family tree and family history.

1. Call a few students up front to sign similar narratives about their own family histories. Have them tell when their parents, grandparents or other relatives came to America, how they met, and the different places they lived.

   Encourage students to practice different kinds of when clauses, and to end their narratives with the sign UP-TILL-NOW.

   They should follow the narrative sequence on the board from the previous activity.

2. Divide the class into small groups to practice narrating their family histories to each other. Encourage students to be active listeners.

BREAKAWAY

TO TELL THE TRUTH
(see Appendix, p. 104)

Purpose: To develop language fluency in the context of cooperative group discussion.

INTERACTION

Biographies

Purpose: To continue practicing when clauses, sequencing events, and family history vocabulary.

1. Tell students to do research on famous Deaf individuals. Each student should work with a partner and select one name from the lists below. The lists are divided according to where reference information can be found; relevant page numbers in each of the reference books are listed after the Deaf person's name.

from *Notable Deaf Persons**

Laurent Clerc (pp. 3 – 4)
Sophia Fowler Gallaudet (pp. 29 – 31)
Melville Ballard (pp. 133 – 136)
Granville Redmond (pp. 160 – 162)

from *Deaf Heritage***

Edwin A. Hodgson (p. 65)
Edmund Booth (p. 67)
Job Turner (p. 68)
Theophilus d'Estrella (pp. 110 – 111)
Regina Olson Hughes (pp. 120 – 121)
Douglas Tilden (pp. 144 – 145)
Laura Searing (p. 194; see also
    Notable Deaf Persons, pp. 7 – 8)

Have each pair of students develop a narrative highlighting significant events in the Deaf person's life. Have students follow the narrative sequence practiced earlier in this unit.

2. After each pair has prepared their narrative, divide the class into two large groups: have partners split up and join different groups so that they each tell their narrative to half the class. In this way the whole class can learn about the same people.

STUDENT VIDEOTEXT AND WORKBOOK

1. Make sure students complete the video-interactive and other activities for this unit, either in class or for homework. Also assign the Culture/Language Notes for this unit.

End of Unit 15

---

*Guilbert C. Braddock, *Notable Deaf Persons*, Gallaudet College Alumni Association, Washington, D.C., 1975.
**Jack R. Gannon, *Deaf Heritage: A Narrative History of Deaf America*, National Association of the Deaf, Silver Spring, MD, 1981.

APPENDIX

BUILDING BLOCKS

1. Bring a set of children's wooden blocks to class and describe the size and shape of each kind of block, i.e., short cylinder, long cylinder, square, rectangle. Review the non-manual markers "oo", "mm" and "cha".

2. Place two *similar* blocks on the table as shown below:

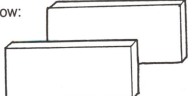

First describe the blocks with DCLs:

> **T:** 2, DCL*"rectangle on the left"*, DCL*"rectangle on the right"*.

Then, show their relationship to each other:

> **T:** (2h)LCL:B*"one behind the other"*.

Continue setting up blocks as shown below, then use locative classifiers to show how the blocks are arranged.

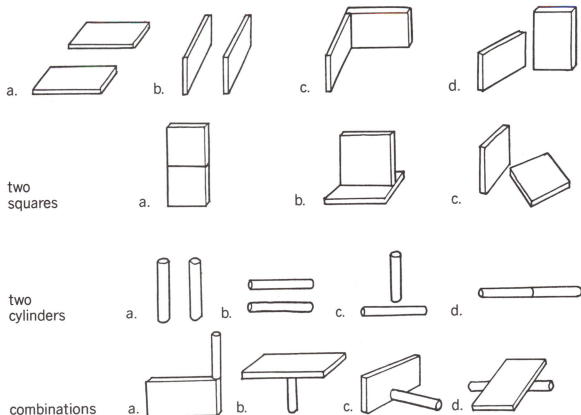

a.   b.   c.   d.

two squares   a.   b.   c.

two cylinders   a.   b.   c.   d.

combinations   a.   b.   c.   d.

3. **Describing the sequence of building**: Call a student up front. Instruct the student to arrange the blocks as you describe them.

First, tell the student which blocks to use:

> **T:** 1 DCL *"rectangle"*, 1 DCL *"cylinder"*, 1 DCL *"square"*.

Show the location of the first block:

>   t̄
> **T:** DCL *"rectangle"*, LCL:B *"on table"*.

Next, representing the first block with the weak hand, tell where to place the second block:

>   t̄
> **T:** DCL *"cylinder"*, [(wh)LCL:B/LCL:1 *"cylinder on B"*].

Then use the weak hand to represent the second block, and tell where to place the third block:

>   t̄
> **T:** DCL *"square"*, [(wh)LCL:1/LCL:B *"square on cylinder"*].

After the student arranges the blocks, ask the class to repeat the sequence above to practice using both the weak hand and the dominant hand.*

4. Continue calling other students up front and have them arrange the blocks according to your description. Describe the following arrangements:

a.   b.   c.

5. Set up a barrier in the middle of the table, then call two students up front. Tell one student to build a configuration of blocks without letting the other student see it. Then have the student sign step-by-step instructions for the other student to build an identical configuration.**

Afterwards, remove the barrier and let students compare the two sets of blocks.

*****NOTE:** Be sure students switch from the dominant hand to the weak hand when showing the previously placed object as a reference point or base for the central (or "new") object.

******NOTE:** Student[1] should give instructions based on how s/he sees the configuration (i.e., the signer's perspective), and Student[2] should build from the same perspective. That is, if Student[1] places an object on his/her right, Student[2] should also place the object on his/her own right.

6. If there are enough blocks to pass around, divide the class into pairs or small groups and have students practice giving instructions while another student builds according to the instructions.

Start with a limited number of blocks, then as students become more proficient, allow them to build more elaborate configurations.

Check students' sign production in the following areas: topic-comment structure, appropriate pausing and use of space, and the switch from dominant to weak hand to show a reference point for the location of the next central object.

NUMBERS

Dates and Addresses

1. Hand out the "Dates and Addresses" worksheets (see Materials Appendix, pp. 107–108). Increase students' comprehension skills by describing events one by one, then spelling out the date for that event:

event	date
U.S. Independence Day	July 4, 1776
attack on Pearl Harbor	Dec. 7, 1941
first American orbital flight around the earth	Feb. 20, 1962
bombing of Hiroshima	Aug. 6, 1945
statehood for Hawaii	Aug. 21, 1959
statehood for Alaska	Jan. 3, 1959
Martin Luther King's birthdate	Jan. 15, 1929
John F. Kennedy assassinated	Nov. 22, 1963
Abraham Lincoln assassinated	April 14, 1865
first person to set foot on the moon	July 20, 1969

Students should write each date next to the corresponding event on their worksheets.

Explain that four consecutive digits (i.e., years) are signed as two two-digit numbers. Model a few examples:

1496: 14+96   1927: 19+27   1968: 19+68   1502: 15+02

Then, describe the above events again and ask students when they occurred. Students should refer to their worksheets and practice spelling out the dates.

Have a transparency of the worksheet ready with the dates filled out so that students can check their answers.

2. Describe different eras and events, and have students fill in the years on their worksheets:

era	years
Russian Revolution	1915 THEREABOUTS
Roaring 20's	1920'S
hippie era	1960'S
Depression	1930'S
Civil Rights Movement	1960'S
California Gold Rush	1849
American Revolution	1775
Boston Tea Party	1773

Use this structure to tell about the general mood or events of an approximate time:

1935 1920'S 1915 1940'S etc.	THEREABOUTS	(describe mood or events)

Sample sentences:

1915 THEREABOUTS RUSSIA REBEL MESS-UP.
1920'S THEREABOUTS PEOPLE HAVE-GAY-LIFE.

Then, describe the above events again and ask students when they occurred. Students should refer to their worksheets and practice spelling out the dates.

3. Sign the information below and have students fill in their worksheets.

event	years
Reconstruction (after Civil War)	1865 – 1877
Hundred Years' War (France and England)	1337 – 1453
Black Plague (Europe)	1347 – 1350
George Washington's life	1732 – 1799
BART* construction	June 1964 – Sept. 1972
Carter presidency	1976 – 1980

Introduce structures to describe a period of time from one point to another, i.e., 1941 – 1945:

(person)	BORN (year), DIED (year)
(event)	START (month/year), FINISH (month/year)
	(year) TILL (year)

Sample sentences:

fs-GEORGE WASHINGTON BORN 1732, DIED 1799.
fs-BART* START BUILDING fs-JUNE 1964, FINISH fs-SEPT 1972.
fs-CARTER PRESIDENT 1976 TILL 1980.

Then, describe the above events again and ask students when they occurred. Students should refer to their worksheets and practice spelling out the dates.

***NOTE:** Acronym for Bay Area Rapid Transit (San Francisco Bay Area).

4. Sign a series of addresses and have students write them on their worksheets:

<u>three-digit numbers</u>
654 Main St.
304 Bush Way
111 East 14th St.
729 21st Ave.
410 Rome Court

Explain that three consecutive digits are signed as the first digit alone, then the last two as a two-digit number.* (Also, the palm always faces outward, except for numbers 11 – 15.) For example:

393: 3+93

Then continue to sign addresses for students to write on their worksheets:

<u>four-digit numbers</u>
4144 Willow Way
2408 Linda Court
5417 45th Ave.
2033 22nd St.

Explain that four consecutive digits for addresses are also signed as two two-digit numbers. Model a few examples:

1438: 14+38
1719: 17+19
1922: 19+22
1507: 15+07

Give more addresses and zip codes for students to write on their worksheets:

<u>five-digit numbers</u>	<u>zip codes</u>
43551 Rose Drive	94102
19003 Green Blvd.	20770
38705 40th St.	10003
42075 5th Ave.	95154
	14620

Explain that addresses or zip codes with five consecutive numbers are signed as a cluster of the first three digits followed by a two-digit number, i.e.:

34316: 3+4+3+16
94704: 9+4+7+04

5. For additional practice, tell some of your family's and friend's addresses, or your former addresses. Have students write down the information and compare it with your master list.

Have students spell out their addresses to each other. Other students should write down the signer's name and address.

---

*NOTE: There are some exceptions, especially with two or more of the same number in a row. In that case, each digit is usually spelled out, i.e: 111 = 1+1+1 (with the palm facing out).

TO TELL THE TRUTH

1. Divide the class into groups of five. Tell students that they must each come up with one statement about themselves. However, within each group only one person's statement should be true; the other four should be lies.

   Give students time to prepare their statements and discuss strategy within each group. The goal is to make even the most outrageous statements seem believable, so that the rest of the class can't tell who is telling the truth.

2. Call up each group in turn to tell their statements to the rest of the class. After the group has finished, the other students try to figure out which statement is true.

   Encourage discussion and disagreement among class members about why one statement or another could or could not be true. You may want to introduce the signs LIE++, FICTIONAL, and "pshaw" for this activity.

   Then have the class vote on who is telling the truth.

3. The group should then announce who is telling the truth.

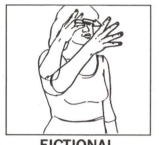

FICTIONAL

DATES AND ADDRESSES
(for p. 101)

Worksheet

Directions: In Parts I – III, your teacher will identify events or eras and tell you their dates or years. Write the dates/years in the appropriate blank. In Part IV, write down the addresses and zip codes your teacher tells you.

Part I

bombing of Hiroshima   _____

John F. Kennedy assassinated   _____

statehood for Hawaii   _____

U.S. Independence Day   _____

attack on Pearl Harbor   _____

first American orbital flight
   around the earth   _____

statehood for Alaska   _____

Martin Luther King's birthdate   _____

Abraham Lincoln assassinated   _____

first person to set foot
   on the moon   _____

Part II

Civil Rights Movement   _____

hippie era   _____

California Gold Rush   _____

Russian Revolution   _____

Boston Tea Party   _____

Depression   _____

Roaring 20's   _____

American Revolution   _____

Part III

	beginning	ending
Reconstruction (after Civil War)	_____	_____
Hundred Years' War (France and England)	_____	_____
Black Plague (Europe)	_____	_____
George Washington's life	_____	_____
San Francisco Bay Area Rapid Transit (BART) construction	_____	_____
Carter presidency	_____	_____

Part IV

1) three-digit numbers

_____

_____

_____

_____

_____

2) four-digit numbers

_____

_____

_____

_____

_____

3) five-digit numbers

_____

_____

_____

_____

_____

4) zip codes

_____

_____

_____

_____

_____

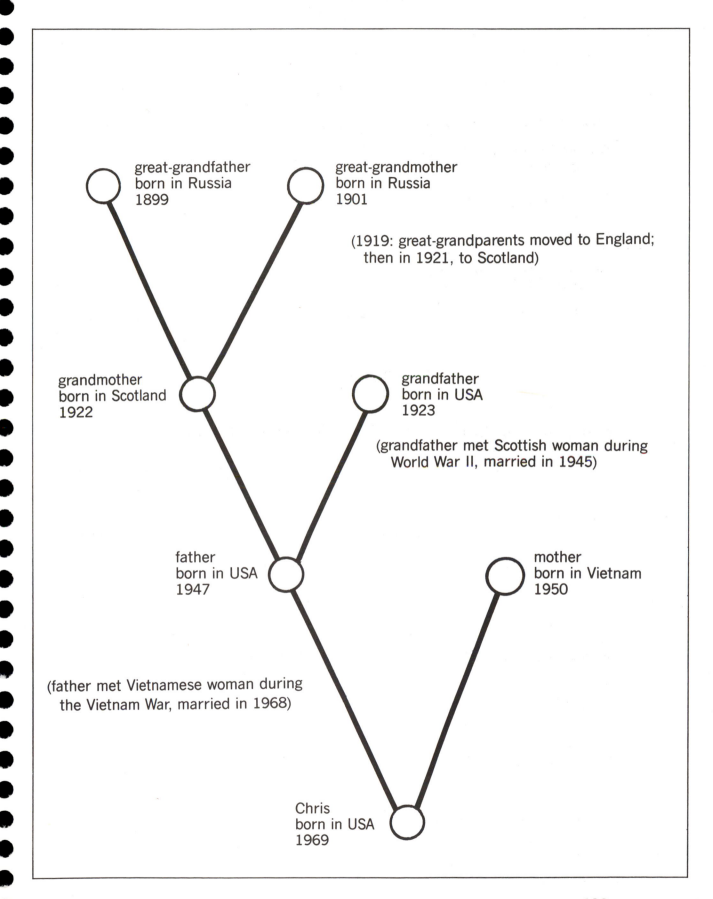

great-grandfather
born in Russia
1899

great-grandmother
born in Russia
1901

(1919: great-grandparents moved to England;
then in 1921, to Scotland)

grandmother
born in Scotland
1922

grandfather
born in USA
1923

(grandfather met Scottish woman during
World War II, married in 1945)

father
born in USA
1947

mother
born in Vietnam
1950

(father met Vietnamese woman during
the Vietnam War, married in 1968)

Chris
born in USA
1969

UNIT 16

DESCRIBING AND IDENTIFYING THINGS

O V E R V I E W

DIALOGUE FORMAT:

Signer A: ask what a word means
B: give definition

SAMPLE DIALOGUE:

$$\overline{\text{whq}}$$
Signer A: fs-FEZ, #WHAT+THAT-ONE.
B: HAT, POSS fs-ARAB, DCL*"short cylindrical cap"* WITH DCL*"tassel from top, hanging on side"*.

VOCABULARY:

materials	food-related signs	opinions of food	meals
WOOD	food signs for specific dishes	VOMIT	EAT+MORNING
METAL	MASH	#EEK	EAT+NOON
RUBBER	BOIL	GREASY	EAT+NIGHT
fs-PLASTIC	BAKE	BITTER	
GLASS	FRY/COOK	!SPICY-HOT!	money numbers: $1.01 to $9.99
FABRIC	fs-FRY	!SWEET!	(#)+DOLLAR for multiples of 5
PAPER	MIX	TASTE AWFUL	time signs for different
fs-CLAY	ICL*"fold"*	STRANGE	frequencies (Breakaway)
fs-CERAMIC	fs-POACH		

SENTENCE STRUCTURES:

describe object

(name of object)	(material)	DCL*"shape, size, texture, design"* (color)	ICL*"how to handle object"*

ask what a word means

$$\overline{\text{whq}}$$ fs-(word), #WHAT+THAT-ONE

define by how it looks

KNOW [POSS (origin)]	$$\overline{}\text{t}$$ fs-NOODLE HAT (furniture)	$$\overline{}\text{nod}$$ DCL [ICL] [THAT-ONE]

define tool

KNOW	$$\overline{}\text{t}$$ [ALMOST SAME-AS (other tool)]	$$\overline{}\text{nod}$$ DCL*"tool"* ICL*"use tool"* [FOR (purpose)] [THAT-ONE]

define toy

_____t_____	_____nod_____
KNOW fs-TOY, DCL*"describe toy"*, [ICL*"use toy"*], [THAT-ONE]	

define appliance

_____t_____	_____nod_____
KNOW (describe function) DCL*"appliance"* [ICL*"use appliance"*] [THAT-ONE]	

describe food by how it is made

(which meal) (origin of dish)	(main ingredient) (type of food)	DCL LCL ICL	(added ingredient)	ICL LCL DCL

GRAMMAR:

descriptive classifiers for shapes, patterns, textures
instrument classifiers
weak hand as reference
topic-comment structure
non-manual markers: "oo", "mm", "cha"

SIGN ILLUSTRATIONS:

DCL:claw*"sphere"* (see p. 112)
DCL:curved-L*"disk"* (see p. 112)
DCL:B↔S*"cone"* (see p. 112)
DCL*"cylinder"* (see p. 112)
DCL:B*"cube"* (see p. 112)
non-manuals: oo, mm, cha (see p. 113)
ONCE-IN-A-LONG-TIME (see Breakaway, p. 131)

MATERIALS:

"Shapes," "Symmetrical Combinations," "Assymmetrical Combinations," "Press, Pull and Open"
  and "Objects" transparencies
"Noodles, Hats and Furniture" worksheet and teacher's key
"Tools, Toys and Appliances" worksheet and teacher's key
Survey Form and Survey Cards (Breakaway)
Merchandise sheets
"Reveille" article

The American Sign Language Handshape Game Cards
stopwatch

INTRODUCTION
Describing Shapes

1. Show the "Shapes" transparency (see Materials Appendix, p. 133). Write on the board:

---

1) describe shapes

---

2. Introduce the appropriate descriptive classifier (DCL) for each shape.*

   Have students imitate each classifier.

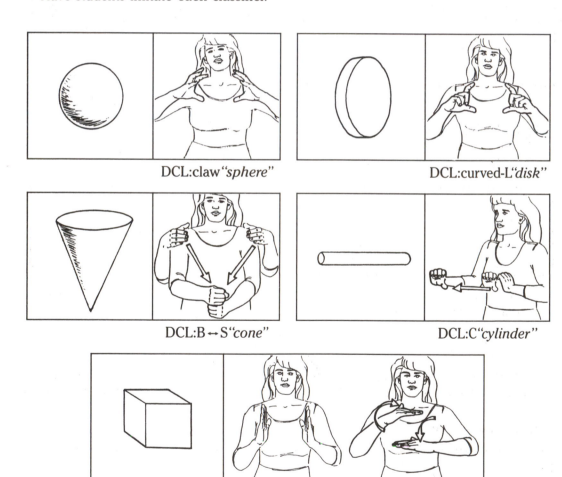

DCL:claw *"sphere"*   DCL:curved-L *"disk"*

DCL:B ↔ S *"cone"*   DCL:C *"cylinder"*

DCL:B *"cube"*

NOTE: When describing objects that are flat, use your index finger(s) to trace the shape. When describing objects that have depth, use the B, C, claw, or other handshapes to show three-dimensionality. Look at the shapes as you describe them.

3. Add to the board:

> *1) describe shapes*
> **a) sizes**

Describe the shapes again, this time varying the size from very small to **very large**. Be sure to use appropriate non-manual markers to indicate size:

"oo" for very small, thin, narrow, etc.
"mm" for average or medium size
"cha" for very large, wide, tall, etc.

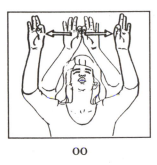
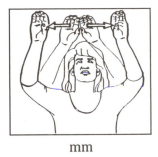

oo   mm   cha

Again have students imitate the classifiers and non-manual markers.

4. Add to the board:

> *1) describe shapes*
> *a) sizes*
> **b) from different perspectives**

Tell students they should imagine they are actually looking at an object as they describe it. Demonstrate how to describe a shape as if you were:

- looking up at it
- looking down at it
- looking around it
- looking inside or through it

Have students imitate your descriptions of shapes from the different perspectives. Then have them vary the size of the shape as they describe it from different perspectives.

5. Add to the board:

> *1) describe shapes*
> *a) sizes*
> *b) from different perspectives*
> **2) describe patterns on objects and surfaces**

Show how to describe the following patterns or designs on various objects and surfaces. Use the sentence structure below. Have students imitate your descriptions.

describe pattern or design

DCL*"object"*	[(wh)DCL*"object"*/DCL*"pattern or design"*]*

pattern/design   sample objects
DCL*"plaid"*   plaid sofa cushion
DCL*"speckled"*   speckled bird egg
DCL*"polka dots"*   dunce cap with polka dots
DCL*"flowery"*   lamp shade with flowery design
DCL*"striped"*   striped gift-wrapped box
DCL*"one line on it"*   dinner plate with one line around it
DCL*"one band around it"*   handcrafted Italian ceramic bowl
DCL*"two lines on it"*   drinking glass with two thin red lines near the top
DCL*"two bands on it"*   tall cylindrical vase with two bands around it
DCL*"zigzag"*   zigzag design on Indian basket
DCL*"spiral"*   candy cane

pattern/design   sample surfaces
DCL*"plaid"*   plaid couch
DCL*"speckled"*   soundproof tiles on ceilings and walls
DCL*"polka dots"*   polka-dotted gift box
DCL*"flowery"*   wallpaper with flower design
DCL*"striped"*   cabana or tent
DCL*"one band"*   solid yellow line in middle of road

Variation: Describe objects that have different patterns or designs on each surface, for example:

• a pillow with one solid side and one striped side
• a box with a different color on each side and polka dots on the top and bottom
etc.

6. Add to the board:

> *1) describe shapes*
>   *a) sizes*
>   *b) from different perspectives*
> *2) describe patterns on objects and surfaces*
> ***3) describe textures of objects***

*****NOTE:** When describing the pattern or design on an *object*, your weak hand should retain the DCL handshape as a reference point. Then the design can be traced over the object with the dominant hand. It is sometimes better to use both hands when describing the pattern or design on a *surface*.

Use the following sentence structure to describe different textures of objects:

describe texture

DCL"*object*"	DCL"*texture*" *

texture   sample objects

puff cheeks
DCL"*bumpy*"   rock wall, iguana

th
DCL"*dented*"   banged-up pots and pans

th
DCL"*warped*"   wood floor warped from dampness

oo
DCL"*very smooth*", ECL"*shiny*"   lacquered jewelry box, crystal ball

tight lips
DCL"*very solid*"   steel ball, weights

puff cheeks
DCL"*soft*"   pillows, clouds

oo
DCL"*fuzzy*"   rabbit's ear, peach

Have students practice signing the different textures on various objects.

7. Add to the board:

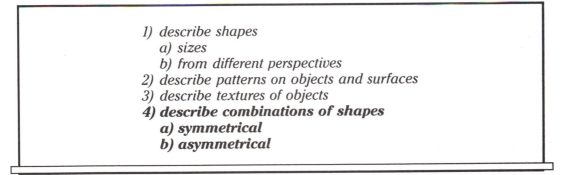

> *1) describe shapes*
> *a) sizes*
> *b) from different perspectives*
> *2) describe patterns on objects and surfaces*
> *3) describe textures of objects*
> **4) describe combinations of shapes**
> **a) symmetrical**
> **b) asymmetrical**

Show the "Symmetrical Combinations" transparency (see Materials Appendix, p. 134). Demonstrate how to sign different combinations, first signing the base shape, then adding the attachments with both hands.** For example:

* point to the cube then point to the cylindrical handles on the transparency
* describe the cube, then with both hands describe the cylindrical handles *on* the cube
* have students repeat after you
* point to the rectangular handles on the transparency
* describe the cube, then with both hands describe the rectangular handles on the cube
* have students repeat after you

---

* **NOTE:** Descriptions of textures are usually signed with *both* hands after the description of the object.
** **NOTE:** Be aware of your use of space: make sure you sign the attachment in the correct location in relation to the base shape.

Continue this procedure until you have demonstrated how to sign all six shapes of attachments, i.e.:

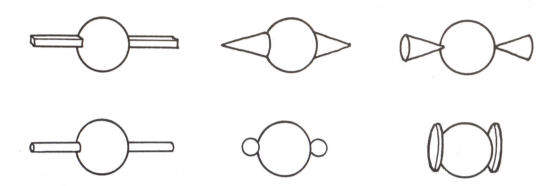

Then point to different base shapes and attachments, and have students describe them.

8. Show the "Asymmetrical Combinations" transparency (see Materials Appendix, p. 135). Demonstrate how to sign several combinations: first sign the base shape, then **keep the weak hand in place** for spatial reference as you describe the attachment.* Follow this procedure:

   • point to the first picture on the transparency
   • describe the base shape, then add the attachment, describing it while keeping your weak hand in place for reference
   • have students repeat after you

   After demonstrating various combinations, point to different pictures on the transparency and have students practice describing the shapes. Make sure they always keep one hand in place for spatial reference,* and that they sign the attachment in the correct location in space.

   Variation: Introduce or review the following vocabulary:

WOOD	METAL	RUBBER	fs-PLASTIC	GLASS
FABRIC	PAPER	fs-CLAY	fs-CERAMIC	(colors)

   Then select several combinations on the transparency and sign sentences like the following:

   WOOD DCL*"sphere"*, [(wh)DCL*"sphere"*/METAL DCL*"handle on right side"*].

   $$\overline{\rule{2cm}{0pt}}^{\,t} \qquad \overline{\rule{7cm}{0pt}}^{\,t}$$
   DCL*"cube"* fs-PLASTIC, [(wh)DCL*"cube"*/DCL*"spherical attachment"*] RUBBER.

---

* **NOTE:** If an object has an attachment on your non-dominant side, use your *dominant* hand to hold a reference point while using your weak hand to describe the attachment.

9. Add to the board:

```
        1) describe shapes
           a) sizes
           b) from different perspectives
        2) describe patterns on objects and surfaces
        3) describe textures of objects
        4) describe combinations of shapes
           a) symmetrical
           b) asymmetrical
        5) describe lids, pumps, handles, etc.
```

Show the "Press, Pull and Open" transparency (see Materials Appendix, p. 136). Point to each object pictured and demonstrate how to describe it using DCLs and instrument classifiers (ICLs). Use your weak hand to hold a reference point as you show how to use the lids, pumps, and handles. Have students imitate your descriptions.

━━━ BREAKAWAY

MORE SILLY PUTTY
(see Appendix, p. 130)

Purpose: To practice skills in visualizing and describing objects.

━━━

SIGN PRODUCTION

"Describing Objects"

1. Show the "Objects" transparency (see Materials Appendix, p. 137) and demonstrate how to describe each object:*

object	description
take-out carton	PAPER DCL*"box with folding lids"*, METAL DCL*"handle"*, ICL*"open lids"*
German beer stein	GLASS DCL*"container with handle"*, LCL:B*"lid"* ICL*"hold handle"*
canning jar	GLASS DCL*"container"* METAL DCL*"lid"* ICL*"screw lid on/off"*
radio	DCL*"box"*, ICL*"turn dial"* ICL*"move lever"*

---

* NOTE: Use the following general sequence rules for describing objects with multiple parts (use whichever one applies to the object):
- from general to specific
- from the biggest part to the smallest part/detail
- from the ground to the top
- from the least mobile to the most mobile

music box	WOOD DCL*"box with lid and wind-up key"*, ICL*"wind key"*
ice cream maker	fs-PLASTIC DCL*"bucket"*, METAL DCL*"bar on top"* ICL*"turn crank"*
hand-soap bottle	GLASS DCL*"bottle with hand pump"* ICL*"pump"*
table lamp	GLASS DCL*"base"* FABRIC DCL*"shade"*, ICL*"switch on/off"*
bicycle pump	METAL DCL*"upright cylinder with T-shaped handle"*, ICL*"pump air into tire"*, RUBBER DCL*"hose"*
tool box	METAL DCL*"rectangular box with cover and inside tray"*, ICL*"remove tray"*
flashlight	fs-PLASTIC DCL*"box with handle and switch"*, ICL*"turn on lamp"*
toilet plunger	RUBBER DCL*"dome"*, WOOD DCL*"stick"*, ICL*"use plunger"*

Review by pointing to objects and having students describe them.

2. Describe some of the same objects (or different ones), but this time add descriptions of various patterns, designs or textures. Use this sentence structure:

describe object

DCL*"shape"*	DCL*"pattern, design or texture"*	ICL*"switch, crank, etc."* DCL*"handle, lid, etc."*

Again have students imitate your descriptions.

"What Does It Look Like?"

Purpose: To develop fluency in describing objects.

1. Show the "Objects" transparency again and introduce signs or phrases to identify each object pictured, i.e.:

MUSIC fs-BOX   LIGHT+ICL*"hold flashlight"*
fs-TOOL-BOX   BICYCLE+ICL*"pump"*

2. Model sentences identifying and describing the objects, and have students repeat after you. For example, point to the picture of the lamp and sign this sequence:

> **T:** LIGHT, GLASS DCL*"base and stem"*.
> LIGHT, GLASS DCL*"base and stem"*, FABRIC DCL*"shade"*.
> LIGHT, GLASS DCL*"base and stem"*, FABRIC DCL*"shade"*, DCL*"pleats in shade"*.
> LIGHT, GLASS DCL*"base and stem"*, FABRIC DCL*"shade"*, DCL*"pleats in shade"* ICL*"switch on/off"*. . .

Have students repeat each description.

3. Continue the drill with other objects, describing various materials, sizes, patterns and textures. Add one part of the description at a time, and have students sign the complete sequence.

   Variation: Go through the pictures again, but ask students to come up with different kinds of the same objects, i.e., floor lamp, box kite, commuter cup.

"Distinguishing Similar Objects"

Purpose: To practice distinguishing similar objects by contrasting features and sizes.

1. Tell each student to bring a specific kind of object to class. *Assign the same object to at least four students,* but tell them to bring unusual sizes or designs so that you have a variety of different examples. Types of objects they can bring:

balls	baskets	cups/mugs
boxes	jars	cans
perfume bottles	purses	locks
flashlights	scopes (i.e., binoculars, telescope, kaleidescope)	

2. Place four objects of the same kind on a table. Number them in the order in which they were placed.

1	2	3	4

   Write in numbers one to four on four blank cards, and hand them out to four students. Have one of the students describe the object that corresponds to the number on his/her card. Students should use the following sentence structure:

describe object

(name of object)	(material)	DCL"shape, size, texture, design"* (color)	ICL"how to handle object"

   Ask another student which object was described and check the signer's card to see if the numbers match.

3. Repeat the activity above, but this time, instruct students to first describe *what is not* before describing *what is,* i.e.,

$$\underline{\quad t \quad} \qquad \underline{\quad cha \quad} \quad \underline{\quad neg \quad} \qquad \underline{\quad mm \quad}$$
CUP DCL"*large cup*" "wave-no", DCL"*small cup*".

---

*NOTE: Make sure students emphasize the feature(s) that distinguish that object from the others.

BREAKAWAY

NUMBERS

Money Numbers

Introduce signs for $1.01 to $9.99

For 1 – 9 cents, sign the dollar amount, then sign ZERO and the number of cents. For example:

$6.08: 6-DOLLAR, ZERO 8

For 10 – 99 cents, sign the dollar amount, then the number of cents. For example:

$6.18: 6-DOLLAR, 18

Introduce (#)+DOLLAR for multiples of 5 ($10 and up)

For $10 – 99.00, sign the number then the sign DOLLAR.

INTRODUCTION

Defining Something by How It Looks

1. Write on the board:

> *Signer A:* ask what a word means
> *B:* give definition:
> * **by how it looks**
>
> | noodles | hats | furniture |
> |---|---|---|
> | mafalde | sombrero | chaise |
> | rigatoni | shako | armoire |
> | fusilli | beret | sideboard |
> | ziti | montera | étagère |
> | penne | fedora | commode |
> | manicotti | fez | tansu |

2. Hand out the "Noodles, Hats and Furniture" worksheets to students and use the teacher's key for reference (see Materials Appendix, pp. 138 – 139).

First role play both Signers A and B, demonstrating how to define the first word in each category by how it looks. For example:

---

                                                      whq
A: fs-(word), **#WHAT+THAT-ONE.**

                                                 t
B: (for mafalde) KNOW++ POSS ITALIAN fs-NOODLE,

                                     t   nod
DCL*"narrow, flat, wavy noodle"* ALMOST SAME-AS fs-LASAGNE, THAT-ONE.

                                                 t
B: (for sombrero) KNOW POSS MEXICO HAT DCL*"wide brim, tall crown"*,
                   nod
THAT-ONE.

                                               t
B: (for chaise) KNOW CHAIR DCL*"shape of chaise"* WITH DCL*"arm rests"*,
                   nod
THAT-ONE.

Students should find the illustration on the worksheet that best matches your description, and fill in the blank with the appropriate word.

3. Call up a student to take your place as Signer B. Tell the other students to **ask** Signer B for a definition of one of the words from the list. Signer B should **refer to** the teacher's key, and define the word by how it looks.

Make sure students use the following structures:

ask what a word means

                                 whq
fs-(word), #WHAT+THAT-ONE

define by how it looks

	t	nod
KNOW [POSS (origin)]	fs-NOODLE HAT (furniture)	DCL [ICL] [THAT-ONE]

Students who missed the first student's question should ask that student (*not* you or Signer B) to repeat the fingerspelled word.

4. Continue the activity until students have filled in their worksheets.

Defining Something by How It Works

1. Add the phrase "by how it works" to the dialogue format on the board. Change the word lists as follows:

Signer A: ask what a word means
   B: give definition
     • *by how it looks*
     • **by how it works**

tools		toys		simple appliances	
slix	*ench*	*groot*	*jout*	*zebo*	*draggant*
frammel	*warrow*	*queeze*	*glith*	*hashet*	*toncho*
oxter	*prillad*	*sittan*	*colpha*	*oogonal*	*meedi*

Explain that you are using invented names of objects rather than the real names so that students will not, in fact, know what the words mean. Hand out the "Tools, Toys and Appliances" worksheets to students and use the teacher's key for reference (see Materials Appendix, pp. 140–141).

2. Conduct this activity in the same way as the activity above. First, role playing both Signers A and B, demonstrate how to define the first word in each category, i.e.:

---

                                  whq
A: fs-(word) #WHAT+THAT-ONE.

                                          t
B: (for "slix") KNOW ALMOST SAME-AS HAMMER, DCL*"slix"* ICL*"use mallet"*,
         nod
THAT-ONE.

                          t   nod
B: (for "groot") KNOW fs-TOY DCL*"groot"* ICL*"hold and push"*, THAT-ONE.

                                    t
B: (for "zebo") KNOW ONION ICL*"chop"* LCL*"glass container"* ONION ICL*"put*
                                                 nod
onion in", ICL*"put lid on and twist it shut"*, ICL*"pump to chop"*, THAT-ONE.

Then call on students to role play Signer B, using the teacher's key as reference. Make sure students use these structures for defining tools, toys and appliances:

define tool

		t	nod
KNOW	[ALMOST SAME-AS (other tool)]	DCL*"tool"* ICL*"use tool"* [FOR (purpose)]	[THAT-ONE]

define toy

_____t_____		_____nod_____
KNOW fs-TOY, DCL_"describe toy"_, [ICL_"use toy"_], [THAT-ONE]		

define appliance

KNOW	_____t_____	_____nod_____
	(describe function)	DCL_"appliance"_ [ICL_"use appliance"_] [THAT-ONE]
	EGG ICL_"slice"_	
	CLEAN fs-RUG	
	#TV COPY	
	ONION ICL_"chop"_	
	EGG ICL_"beat"_	
	CARROT ICL_"grate"_	

The rest of the class should ask the meaning of the different words on the board, and fill in their worksheets.

Defining Something by How It Is Made

1. Add the phrase "by how it is made" to the dialogue format on the board:

Signer A: _ask what a word means_
B: _give definition:_
- _by how it looks_
- _by how it works_
- **_by how it is made_**

Ask students about different ways to cook potatoes:

_____t_____	_____q_____	__whq__
T: KNOW POTATO, COOK DIFFERENT++, RIGHT. "what".		

Introduce or review the following vocabulary:

MASH   BOIL   BAKE   FRY/COOK   fs-FRY

Then ask students how they like to cook eggs:

_____t_____	_____q_____	_____whq_____
T: KNOW EGG, COOK DIFFERENT++, RIGHT. HOW COOK, HOW.		

Introduce or review this vocabulary:

BOIL	ICL*"fold"*	fs-POACH
fs-FRY	ICL*"turn over"*	ICL*"stir"* or MIX (scrambled)

2. Show pictures of these foods or write their names on the board:

taco   omelette   banana split

Point to one of the foods and demonstrate how you would define it by describing how it is made. For example:

---

                                                           whq

A: fs-TACO (fs-OMELETTE, fs-BANANA-SPLIT), #WHAT+THAT-ONE.

B: (for taco) MEXICO, fs-TORTILLA DCL*"folded tortilla"*, MEAT, LETTUCE, CHEESE, ONION, TOMATO ICL*"sprinkle"*.

B: (for omelette) EAT+MORNING, EGG DCL:L*"thin disk"* fs-HAM, CHEESE ICL*"sprinkle"*, LCL*"fold over"*.

B: (for banana split) ICE-CREAM LCL:claw*"3 scoops in bowl"*, BANANA DCL*"long thin slices"* LCL*"banana in relation to ice cream"*, CHOCOLATE ICL*"pour over"*, NUTS ICL*"sprinkle"*.

---

3. Add a list of other foods on the board (or show pictures from magazines):

stuffed green peppers
chef's salad
ambrosia
corn dog
stir fry
blintzes

Introduce the vocabulary listed under the name of each dish:

stuffed green peppers

GREEN+fs-PEPPER BOIL
MEAT, ONION, fs-RICE ICL*"mix"*, ICL*"stuff"*
TOMATO ICL*"pour"*

Check students' comprehension and practice vocabulary for stuffed peppers by describing the individual ingredients with DCLs or other signs, and have students give you the right sign. For example:

> **T:** DCL*"small sphere"*, ICL*"chop"*, SMELL CRY++...
>
> **S:** ONION.

Continue introducing and practicing vocabulary for the other food items on the board.

chef's salad

SALAD or fs-CHEF-SALAD
LETTUCE
MUSHROOM
TURKEY
fs-HAM ICL*"chop"*
TOMATO ICL*"slice"*
CHEESE ICL*"grate"*
GREEN ONION
fs-BOIL EGG ICL*"chop"*
ICL*"pour dressing over"*

ambrosia

ORANGE
PINEAPPLE
CHERRY
GRAPE
BANANA
fs-YOGURT
NUT
ICL*"toss in"*
MIX

corn dog

HOT-DOG
fs-CORN+BREAD
ICL*"dip and twirl"*

stir fry

CHINA
CHICKEN
fs-PORK
fs-BEEF
fs-TOFU
CARROT
fs-BROCCOLI
fs-CAULIFLOWER
ONION
MUSHROOM
fs-VEG ICL*"toss in"*, MIX
fs-SOY ICL*"pour"*
(food item) ICL*"slice"*
(food item) ICL*"chop"*
(food item) ICL*"sprinkle"*

blintzes

SAME-AS fs-PANCAKE
CHEESE ICL*"sprinkle"*
ICL*"roll"*
JAM ICL*"spread on"*
fs-POWDER SUGAR ICL*"sprinkle"*
SOUR fs-CREAM ICL*"spoon on"*

After reviewing the vocabulary, have students practice in pairs, asking and telling how to make the different foods on the board. They should use the following sentence structure:

describe food by how it is made

(which meal) (origin of dish)	(main ingredient) (type of food)	DCL LCL ICL	(added ingredient)	ICL LCL DCL

Monitor students for appropriate phrasing and their use of DCLs and ICLs for the different food items.

SIGN PRODUCTION

"My Favorite Food"

Purpose: To practice describing food dishes by how they look and how they are made.

1. Ask students to think of a favorite dish. Have each student describe the dish *without* telling its name. (Make sure each student describes a different dish.) Encourage students to use the sentence structure introduced previously:

describe food by how it is made

(which meal) (origin of dish)	(main ingredient) (type of food)	DCL LCL ICL	(added ingredient)	ICL LCL DCL

Other students must guess what the dish is with signs or fingerspelling. Introduce any new signs that students need to describe or identify different foods.

2. Then ask students to think of a food they hate, and follow the same procedure above.

Encourage students to indicate their dislikes by adding negative non-manual markers and other signs after their descriptions, i.e.:

VOMIT	BITTER	TASTE AWFUL
#EEK	!SPICY-HOT!	STRANGE
GREASY	!SWEET!	

Again have other students guess the food with signs or fingerspelling, and introduce vocabulary as needed.

BREAKAWAY

TAKE A SURVEY
(see Appendix, p. 130)

Purpose: To review activities vocabulary and practice time signs with frequency concepts.

BEAT THE CLOCK
(see Appendix, p. 132)

Purpose: To review vocabulary (increasing awareness of how different signs have similar handshapes), and to encourage students to work as a team.

INTERACTION

Describing Unusual Objects

Purpose: For cumulative practice, students describe unusual objects using DCLs, ICLs and comparisons to common objects.

1. Write on the board:

> *A: tell about something unusual you got*
> > *• tell how it looks*
> > *• tell how it works*
>
> *A/B: continue discussion:*
> > *• how/why A got it*
> > *• what it's used for*
> > *• where s/he keeps it*
> > *etc.*

Role play both Signers A and B in a sample dialogue (i.e., about an old clothes wringer):

```
            cs                                              _____
A: BEFORE, ME GO-TO fs-FLEA-MARKET, BUY !OLD!. . . KNOW CLOTHES
```

```
                                                            _____
DCL"rollers" [(wh)LCL:bent-B"clothes go through rollers"/ICL"turn crank at
     t         nod
side"], THAT-ONE.
```

```
              q         whq
B: REAL/TRUE, WHY BUY.
```

```
    mm
A: ENJOY. LIKE COLLECT OLD, STRANGE THING.
```

```
         whq
B: WHERE PUT.
```

A: EAT+ROOM, CORNER LCL:B*"wringer standing upright in corner"*.

B: OH-I-SEE. LONG-AGO MY GRANDMOTHER HAVE ONE. ME LIKE PLAY [(wh)BCL*"put hand through wringer"*/ICL*"turn crank at same time"*].

```
       neg/q
A: NOT HURT.
```

B: (shake head) NOTHING-TO-IT.

2. Divide the class into pairs to practice the dialogue. Afterwards, students should switch roles and discuss another unusual item.

3. After students have practiced both roles, call up a few students to describe their partner's object to the whole class. Encourage other students to add comments or questions.

Shopping Around

Purpose: To practice describing objects and telling prices.

1. Copy the four Merchandise sheets (see Materials Appendix, pp. 144–147). Select four students to role play store owners 1–4, and give each one a Merchandise sheet.

2. Make two *more* copies of the Merchandise sheets,* and cut out each item. *Make sure you remove the prices.* Distribute the cut-out pictures among the rest of the class who will role play customers. Each customer should have pictures of five to seven items.

3. Review sign forms for money numbers (see Numbers Breakaway, p. 120). Then write on the board:

Object: Customers must find the price for each of their items.

- *Go to a store owner and describe an item specifically (do* not *show your pictures).*
- *If the store owner has it, buy it by writing down the price and the store owner's name.*

---

4. Afterwards, ask questions about the different kinds of items customers bought, i.e.:

- Who bought the cuckoo clock?
- How much did the toaster with four slots cost?
- What kind of saw did you buy?
- Which TV was the cheapest?

---

*NOTE: For larger classes (more than 25), you will have to make more copies of the Merchandise sheets to be sure each customer gets enough items. Or you can divide the class and have two groups of store owners and two groups of customers.

EXTENDED COMPREHENSION

Reveille: Old Wake-Up Devices for Deaf People

1. Tell students how Deaf people of years past found innovative ways to wake themselves up. Describe the various methods and devices used (see Byron B. Burnes's article "Reveille," Materials Appendix, pp. 148–149).

   Test students' comprehension by either asking them to draw the devices as well as they can, or to repeat your descriptions.

2. Afterwards, hand out copies of the article for students to read.

STUDENT VIDEOTEXT AND WORKBOOK

1. Make sure students complete the video-interactive and other activities for this unit, either in class or for homework. Also assign the Culture/Language Notes for this unit.

End of Unit 16

APPENDIX

MORE SILLY PUTTY

1. Have the class sit in a circle. Begin by describing an imaginary ball and bouncing it, then bounce the ball to one of the students in class.

    The student receiving the ball must act out the catch, i.e., if you bounced it hard and fast, the student should respond accordingly.

2. The student who caught the ball must now change it to another shape (for example, hula hoop, frisbee, paper airplane), and show how it is used.

3. After describing the transformation, the student passes the object to another student by rolling, bouncing, or throwing it. The student who catches it then describes another transformation, passes it on appropriately, and so on.

    Make sure students follow the procedure below:

    *   catch the object according to how it should be handled based on size, shape, speed and direction of the throw or bounce
    *   describe a new object
    *   show how it is used
    *   pass it on to another student (vary the speed, strength and direction of the throw or bounce)

TAKE A SURVEY

1. Draw several timelines on the board:

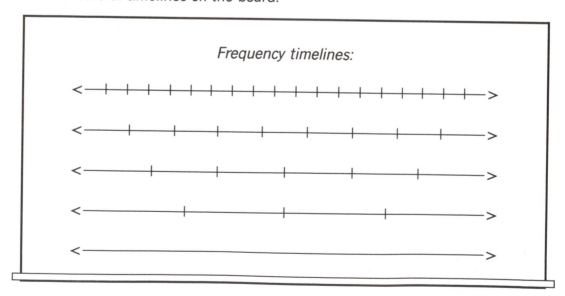

Introduce the following signs to fit each frequency timeline:

 EVERY-HOUR
EVERYDAY
<u>intense</u>
OFFEN
EVERY-(day of the week)
WEEKLY
ONCE+WEEKLY
TWICE+WEEKLY

   <u>so-so</u>
SOMETIMES
EVERY-TWO-WEEKS
MONTHLY

 ONCE-IN-A-WHILE
EVERY-TWO-MONTHS
EVERY-THREE-MONTHS

**ONCE-IN-A-
LONG-TIME**

ONCE-IN-A-LONG-TIME
ONCE+YEAR
EVERY-SIX-MONTHS

 NEVER

2. Demonstrate a sample yes/no question to ask about how often students do various things, i.e.:

q
T: YOU OFTEN GO-TO++ VISIT GRANDMOTHER+GRANDFATHER.

Emphasize that students should respond with YES or #NO and the appropriate vocabulary from the lists above.

3. Divide the class into groups of four students each. Distribute Survey Forms to the whole class, and give a different Survey Card to each student in a group (see Materials Appendix, pp. 142 – 143).

Have students take turns asking the questions on their cards. They should then mark their Survey Forms with the number of students who responded at each degree of frequency.

BEAT THE CLOCK

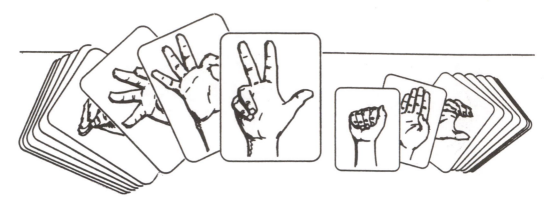

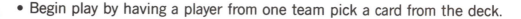

1. **Preparation:** Bring to class cards numbered 1 – 20 of *The American Sign Language Handshape Game Cards** or draw your own. Also bring a stopwatch or ask someone to be timekeeper.

2. **To Play:** Divide the class into teams with the same number of students on each team. Explain the following rules:

   • Begin play by having a player from one team pick a card from the deck.

   • Team members must each in turn come up with a different sign using the handshape on the card.

   • Each team has two minutes to complete two rounds, i.e., if there are five players on a team, the team has two minutes to come up with ten different signs using that handshape.

   • A player cannot skip a turn. Play is suspended until the player thinks of a sign or until the two minutes are up.

   • Team members are not allowed to help each other.

   • Players cannot repeat a sign already given in the same game.

3. **To Score:** Start the clock when the team member chooses the card. As soon as the team has completed two rounds, stop the clock and record the time on the board.

   If the team is not able to complete two rounds within two minutes, stop play and record two minutes on the board for that team.

   Go on to the next team, have a member select a card and repeat the procedure.

4. **To Win:** The team with the lowest total time wins.

**The American Sign Language Handshape Game Cards*, Benjamin J. Bahan and Frank Allen Paul, Dawn Sign Press, Berkeley, CA, 1984.

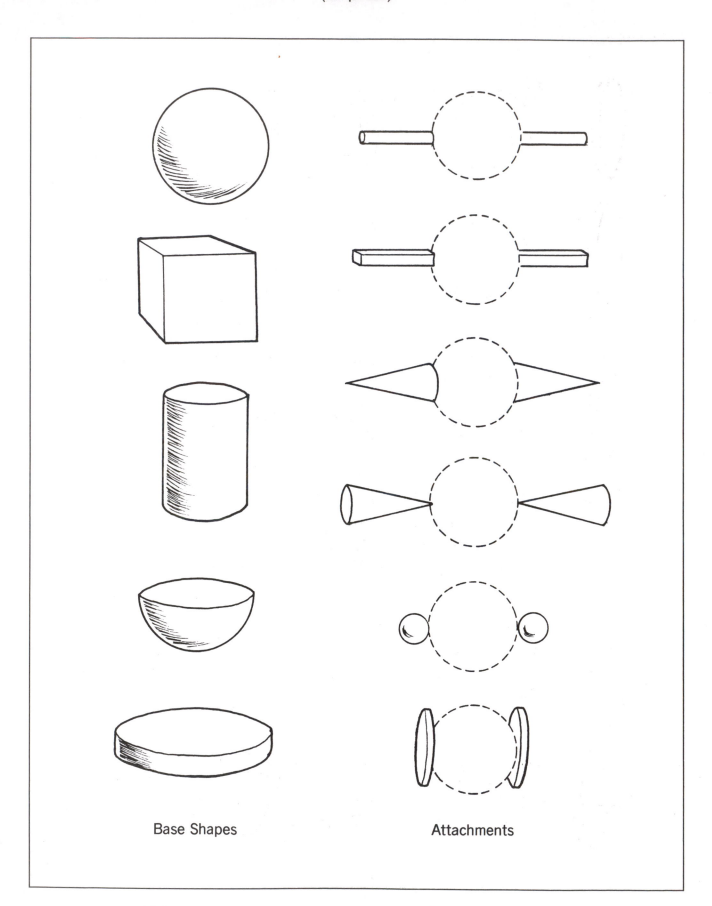

Base Shapes

Attachments

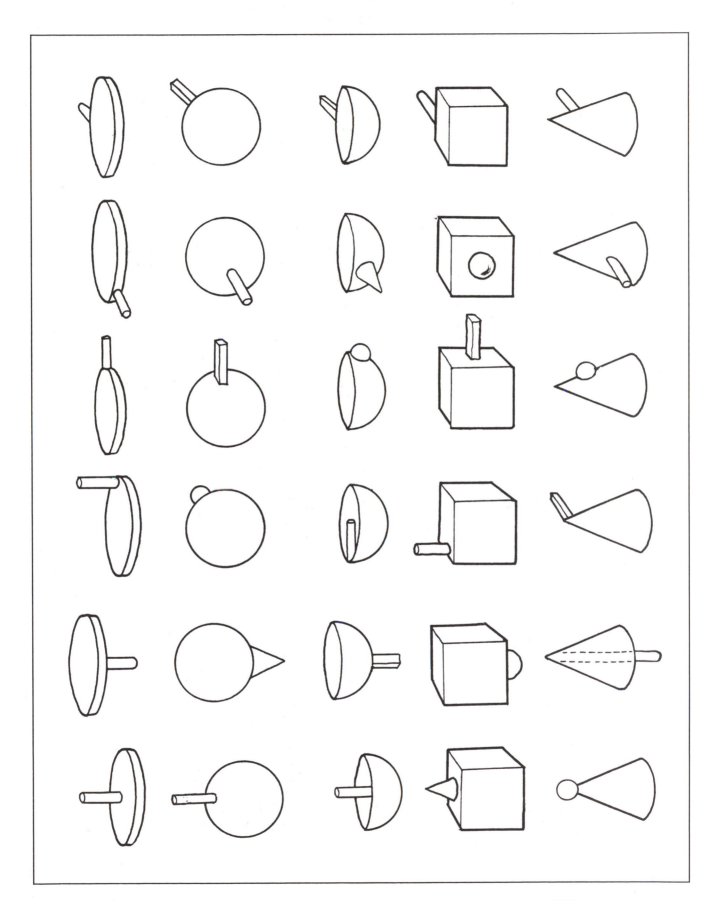

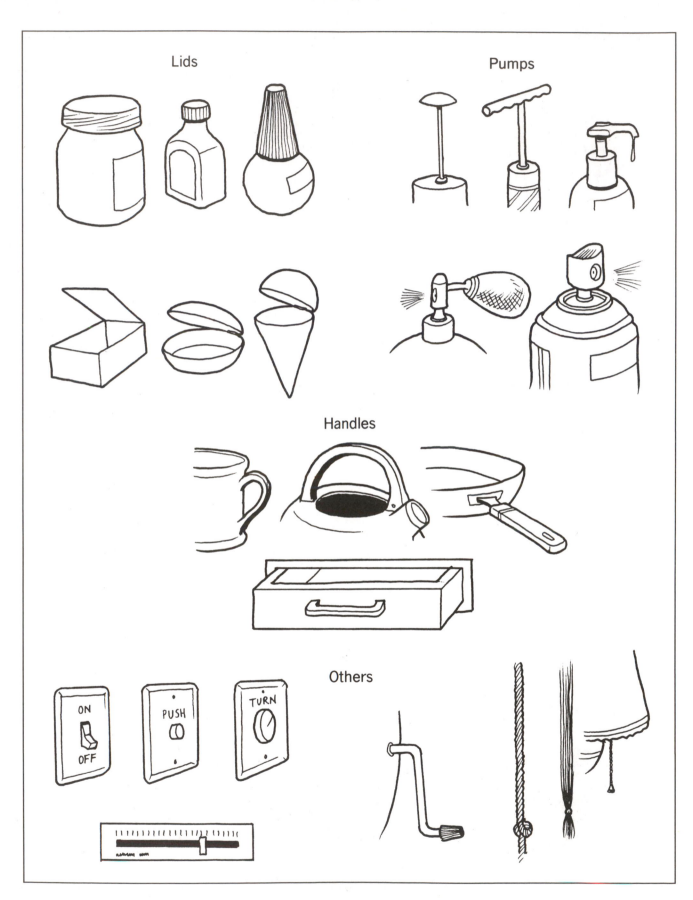

Lids

Pumps

Handles

Others

NOODLES, HATS AND FURNITURE
(for p. 120)
Worksheet

Directions: As each word on the board is defined, find the corresponding picture and write the word below it.

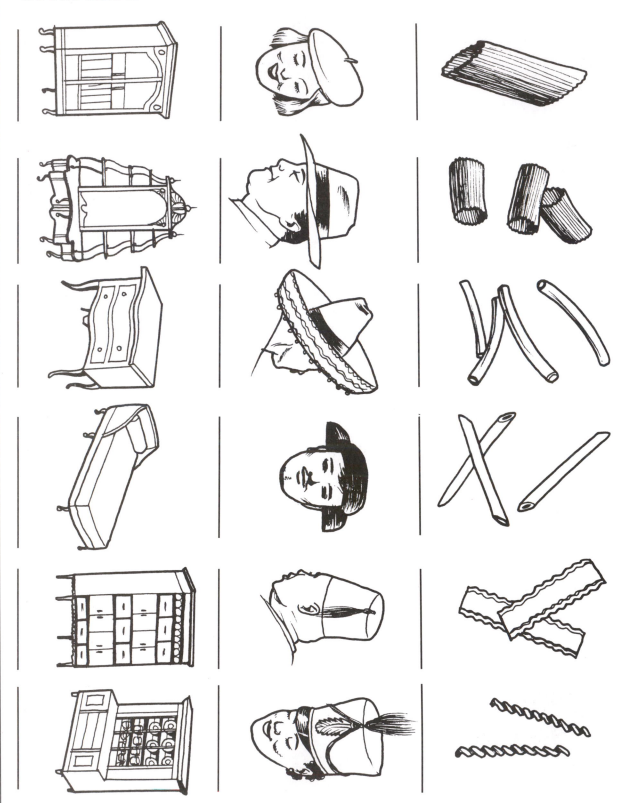

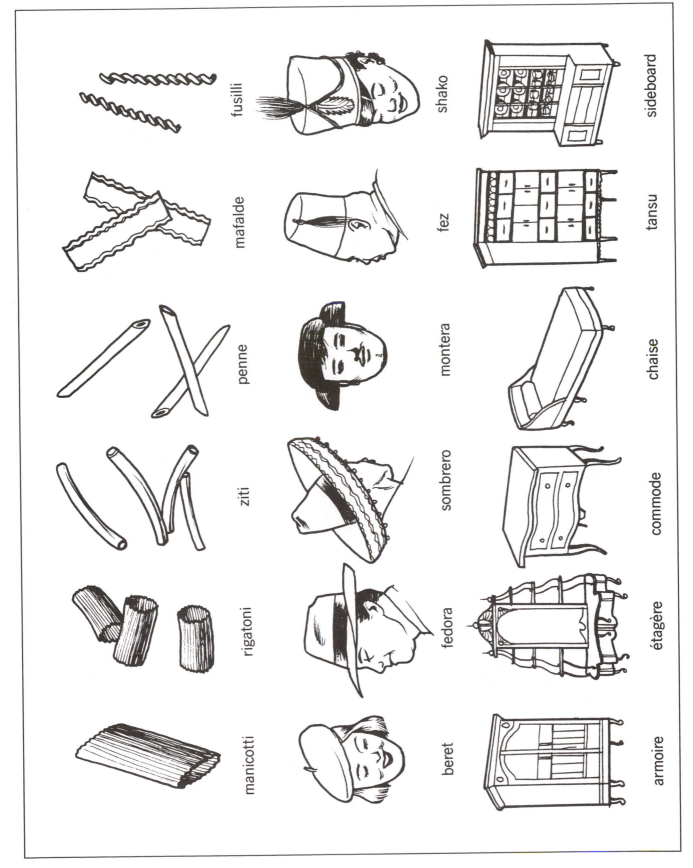

fusilli

shako

sideboard

mafalde

fez

tansu

penne

montera

chaise

ziti

sombrero

commode

rigatoni

fedora

étagère

manicotti

beret

armoire

TOOLS, TOYS AND APPLIANCES
(for p. 122)
Worksheet

Directions: As each word on the board is defined, find the corresponding picture and write the word below it.

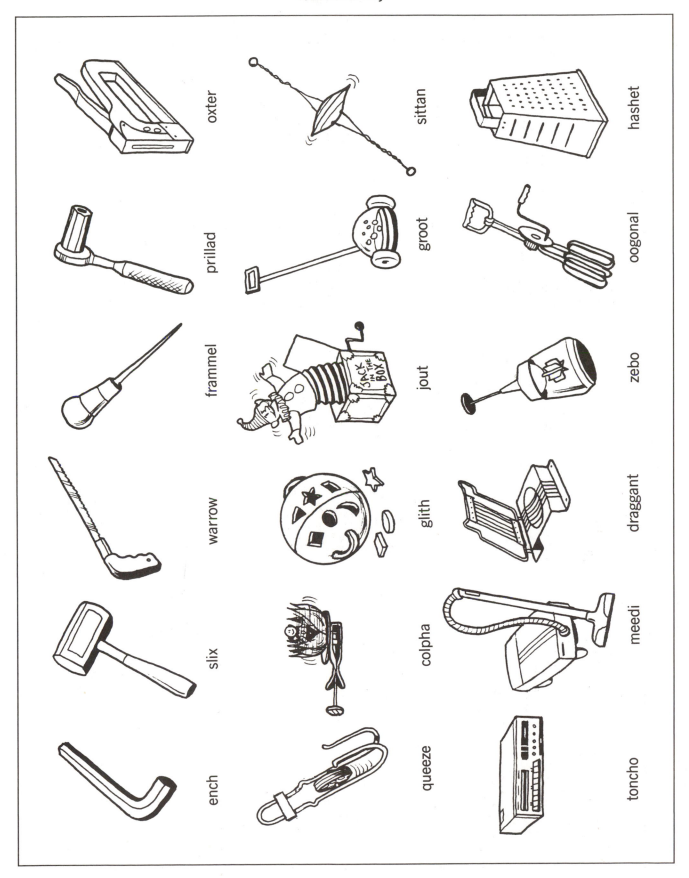

oxter

sittan

hashet

prillad

groot

oogonal

frammel

jout

zebo

warrow

glith

draggant

slix

colpha

meedi

ench

queeze

toncho

SURVEY FORM
(for p. 131)

Directions: Ask the other students in your group how often they do the things on your Survey Card. Mark the number of students who respond at each degree of frequency.

Frequency

<————> <—+—> <—+ +—> <—+++—> <—+++++—>

	<————>	<—+—>	<—+ +—>	<—+++—>	<—+++++—>
Question 1 How many people?	———	———	———	———	———
Question 2 How many people?	———	———	———	———	———
Question 3 How many people?	———	———	———	———	———
Question 4 How many people?	———	———	———	———	———

**Survey Card
Student 1**

How often do you:

1) clean the bathroom at home

2) have a cold

3) cry

4) lend money

5) visit your parents

**Survey Card
Student 2**

How often do you:

1) rearrange your living room or bedroom

2) have indigestion

3) blow up in anger

4) have people over for dinner

5) write letters

**Survey Card
Student 3**

How often do you:

1) change the sheets on your bed

2) go see a doctor

3) have nightmares

4) eat dessert

5) call your aunt or uncle

**Survey Card
Student 4**

How often do you:

1) clean your desk

2) have a hard time sleeping

3) have a good laugh

4) receive flowers

5) kiss

Directions: You own a store that carries only the items pictured below. Customers will come around asking you if you have specific items. Make sure the customer describes the item clearly. If you are not sure you have the right one, ask questions to clarify. When sure, give the price.

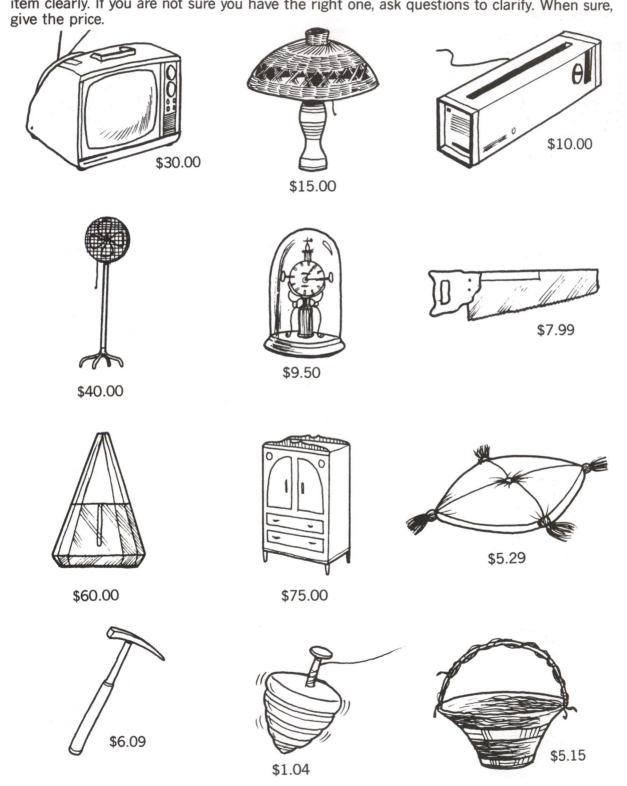

$30.00

$15.00

$10.00

$40.00

$9.50

$7.99

$60.00

$75.00

$5.29

$6.09

$1.04

$5.15

MERCHANDISE
(for p. 128)

Store Owner 2

Directions: You own a store that carries only the items pictured below. Customers will come around asking you if you have specific items. Make sure the customer describes the item clearly. If you are not sure you have the right one, ask questions to clarify. When sure, give the price.

$50.00

$65.00

$25.00

$7.99

$35.00

$20.00

$6.09

$40.00

$9.50

$3.13

$5.29

$1.04

145

Directions: You own a store that carries only the items pictured below. Customers will come around asking you if you have specific items. Make sure the customer describes the item clearly. If you are not sure you have the right one, ask questions to clarify. When sure, give the price.

$75.00

$15.00

$30.00

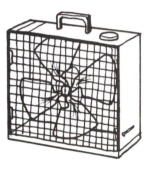

$10.00

$45.00

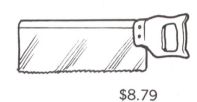

$8.79

$3.25

$60.00

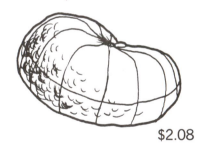

$2.08

$1.55

$4.19

$6.87

Directions: You own a store that carries only the items pictured below. Customers will come around asking you if you have specific items. Make sure the customer describes the item clearly. If you are not sure you have the right one, ask questions to clarify. When sure, give the price.

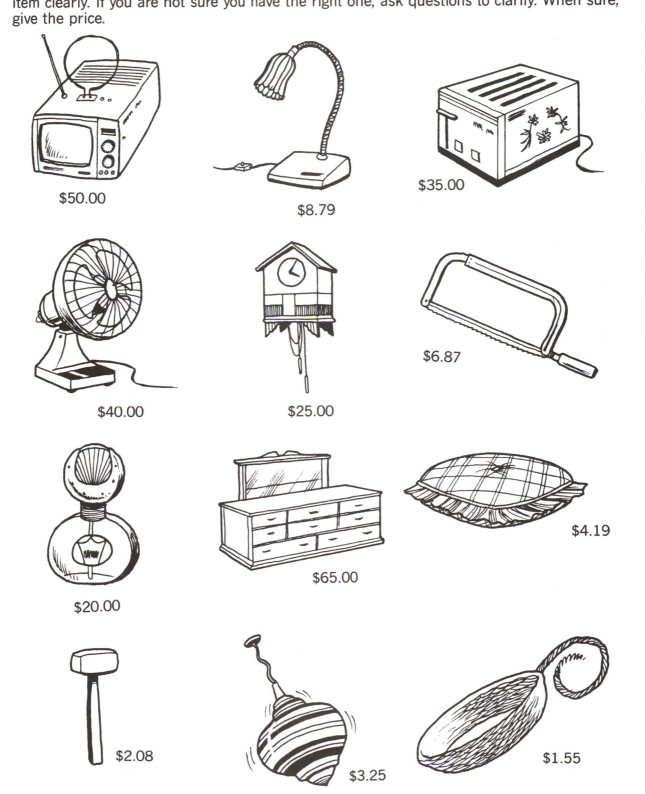

$50.00

$8.79

$35.00

$40.00

$25.00

$6.87

$20.00

$65.00

$4.19

$2.08

$3.25

$1.55

"REVEILLE"
(for p. 129)
by Byron B. Burnes

"I can't get 'em up, I can't get 'em up, I can't get 'em up in the maaaw-ning." That's the song the soldier's bugle is supposed to toot when the crackling notes of reveille rend the morning air. "I can't get 'em up," the bugler wails, but what a task he would have if all his sleeping comrades were deaf!

The efforts of the deaf to keep an appointment with the rosy finger of dawn have resulted in the invention of many weird and wonderful contraptions as auxiliary alarm clock equipment, and it is time now to describe some of them for the benefit of history, before they all vanish in favor of the modern electric radio clock.

One of the gravest problems of the deaf is how to disentangle themselves from the Morpheus headlock exactly at a given time in the morning. That is, it was a problem until the appearance of the radio clock. Nowadays you will find a radio clock in practically every deaf home. It turns on the light in the morning at any time it is asked, and the light will awaken most deaf sleepers. Those who are immune to light have made adaptations for the clock, such as an attachment which will set off a buzzer fastened to the bed. The buzzer causes the bed to vibrate, and if allowed to run long enough, it will start vibrations throughout the bedroom, the living room, the kitchen, the bathroom, and the apartments above and below and across the hall. The deaf sleeper usually awakens before the vibrations cross the street. He awakens amidst the cussing of neighboring apartment dwellers, but, being deaf, he is unaffected by the cuss words — which do not vibrate.

But before the advent of the marvelous radio clock, the deaf really resorted to some fantastic efforts to dispel their slumbers at the proper time.

Among the deaf the nearest approach to the army bugler probably is the supervisor (now better known as counselor) in a school for the deaf. It is his duty to get the pupils out of the sack in time for breakfast. This he accomplishes by shaking every bed, and he delegates some early risers in the dormitory to assist with the bed-shaking. This is effective. It fails only when the supervisor, himself, oversleeps, but supervisors do not oversleep. They have alarm contraptions of their own.

The only supervisor I know who needs no alarm is Louis Byouk, of the California School, who relies solely upon mental determination to get up in the morning. If he wants to get up at five o'clock in the morning, he merely tells himself so the night before, and five o'clock finds him up and smiling. There are other such gifted individuals among the deaf, but they are few and far between.

One time in the early days of my deafness, before I was aware of the alarm contraptions used by the deaf, it became necessary for me to arise at an early hour one morning to meet a train. I took an old-fashioned alarm clock to bed with me, clutched tightly in my hand, and I resolved to keep it clutched. The alarm cut loose at the proper time and I felt the jingling of the bell, and caught my train. Most of us wouldn't care to clutch an alarm clock in our hands through every night for the rest of our lives, however.

During my college days I spent a summer as a hotel employee in the Catskills and I had as partner Al Rose, of Gallaudet football fame. Al is (or was) about the only person in the world who can sleep longer than I can, but as hotel employees we found it necessary to get up early in the morning. The lighting of a water heater was our special responsibility, and we had to have the water hot in time for the earliest riser among the hotel guests.

Rose and I slept in twin cots. I tied an alarm clock securely to the head of my cot and when the alarm sounded in the mornings the vibration was sufficient to arouse me. It wasn't my turn to light the fire every morning, though, so there was still the problem of how to arouse Al on his mornings. Summer mornings in the Catskills are quite chilly, and it was a terrifying ordeal to hop out of my cot each morning and bounce over and waken Al. I solved the problem by running a string from my cot to his. When my alarm sounded, I jerked the string and Al emerged from the covers cussing and fuming in his best fire-lighting form. By the end of the summer I got so I could jerk the string without even waking up.

Some marvelous inventions have been fashioned by deaf sleepers in efforts to enhance the service of alarm clocks, all made possible by the fact that the key with which you wind the alarm also unwinds as the bell rings. The simplest of these inventions is merely connecting this key by a string to the cord that switches on an electric bulb over the bed, in such a manner that when the alarm sounds, the string wraps itself around the unwinding key, tightening sufficiently to pull the light cord far enough to turn on the light. A light suddenly turned on in the face of most deaf sleepers will awaken them.

Nick Braunagel of the North Dakota School has written in his paper, *The Banner*, a description of the kind of alarm he uses. It is so simple, only a genius like Nick could have thought it up. Nick merely connects up his alarm clock with an electric fan and the alarm starts up the fan, which blows across his bed. Lest readers unacquainted with Nick fail to appreciate the potentialities of such a device, it should be pointed out here that Nick sleeps with windows wide open. A fan in his room in the North Dakota winter produces such an icy blast it freezes his snores and hangs them up in mid-air. Nick Braunagel is perhaps the only man in the world who would put up with arising each morning in the face of a blizzard, but Nick's sensibilities are cushioned by his 225 pounds.

There is a story of a deaf man in a Montana mining community who used a flatiron for an alarm. He used a string and pulley arrangement which suspended the flatiron near the ceiling during the night. When morning came his alarm clock would trip a release permitting the iron to drop to the floor. A flatiron falling from the ceiling in the stillness of the morning should waken the deafest of the deaf.

This man's flatiron became a tradition in the village. It could be heard by all the neighbors, and all the miners in town depended upon its faithful boom to start them off to work. Came a day when the owner of the flatiron alarm took unto himself a bride. He took three days off from work and left town for a honeymoon trip. Upon his return he found that there had been no work in the mines for three days. All the miners were blissfully snoring away, awaiting the rousing boom of his flatiron.

When I was teaching in the South Dakota School, one of the pupils, named Horace Todd, had something of a monopoly on making an alarm gadget for deaf persons at the school. His contraption consisted of two slats hinged together, which were attached to the head of the bed. One slat, hanging from the hinge, carried a lead weight on its lower end. It had a hook which made connections with the key on the back of an alarm clock, which sat on a small platform attached to the head of the bed above the two slats. When the alarm sounded, the unwinding key would disengage itself from the hook on the slat, and the slat, with its lead weight, would slam down against its counterpart with a bang like that of a shotgun. The noise, of course, would not awaken a deaf sleeper, but the shock it produced would awaken both the sleeper and the bed beneath him. He made one of his gadgets for me.

Another deaf fellow in South Dakota — Grant Daniels — disengaged himself from the blankets in the mornings to the tune of another kind of alarm, which was used by numerous deaf people in years gone by. This was a sort of box-like arrangement, long and narrow, standing vertically at the head of the bed. Within the box were a number of small shelves, one above the other, sloping gently downward, and on the top shelf rested a small version of a cannon ball, about two inches in diameter, purloined perhaps from the innards of a tractor, where it served as a ball bearing, only, of course, Grant Daniels, a good church man, would not purloin. The ball was held in place on the top shelf by some kind of connection with the alarm key, and when the alarm sounded the key would release the ball. Urged authoritatively by gravity, the ball would roll off the shelf, hit the next one, roll on to the next, and so on until it had bounced off every shelf and come to rest at the bottom of the box. "Bong, bong, bong." Light sleepers would awaken with the first "bong". Those inclined to sleep more soundly might respond to a later bong, but the beauty in this kind of alarm was that it could be constructed to suit individual habits.

The hardest of the sleepers could make the box long enough to extend through the ceiling, enabling it to produce 67 bongs and 4 selahs.

I have heard of an elaboration of the slat contrivance produced by Horace Todd, but I have never seen it. At any rate, in this machine the top slat was supposed to be of the size and shape of an ironing board, and instead of banging against another slat to produce a loud retort, it would slam down right upon the person of the sleeper. If he happened to be too relaxed, there was a possibility that he would wake up in the basement.

When I was a kid at home my mother worked out a means of awakening me which should be commended both for its effectiveness and its simplicity of operation. My bedroom was in a room upstairs above the dining room and my mother did not relish the daily task of climbing the stairs to get me up. She would go into the dining room with a broom and use the broom handle as a sort of battering ram against the ceiling beneath my bed. Since the ceiling was of wood, this created sufficient vibration to waken me.

The most interesting and the most greatly to be desired of all alarm gadgets I have encountered came under my observation during a stay in a hospital. Each morning a beauteous creature immaculately clad in white would enter the room and tap me lightly on the shoulder.

Felix Kowalewski tells me that Heimo Antila had an alarm apparatus which must have been the most Rube Goldbergian of them all. Heimo's alarm was a rat trap, so fastened to the wall that it would pull the light switch when it went off, turning on the light by Heimo's bed. The trap was set off by a string connecting the bait trigger to the unwinding key of an alarm clock. This contraption deserves preservation in the Smithsonian Institute.

There may be other forms of alarms utilized by the deaf, but the kind most commonly used today is the radio clock, mentioned before. In two instances all alarm clocks lose their effectiveness, and the deaf are subject to this failing the same as anyone else. One occasion is when the sleeper responds to the alarm, turns over and shuts it off, and then falls back to sleep. The other instance is when he hops into bed at night, forgetting to set his alarm. The only remedy for these shortcomings is to refrain from going to bed.

*reprinted with author's permission from *The Silent Worker* (now *The Deaf American*), April, 1949.

UNIT 17

TALKING ABOUT THE WEEKEND
O V E R V I E W

DIALOGUE FORMAT:

Signer A: ask about
the weekend
B: respond, describe your
weekend activities
A: comment

SAMPLE DIALOGUE:

$$\overline{\hspace{1.5cm}}^{q}$$

A: WEEK+END ENJOY YOU.

$$\overline{\hspace{1.5cm}}^{t}$$

B: SO-SO, PAST+SATURDAY ALL-DAY ME STAY HOME, CLEANING,
VACUUMING, WASH-CLOTHES CLOTHES, BOX PACKING,

$$\overline{\hspace{2cm}}^{when}$$

PUT-AWAY++ IX-loc*"up"* fs-ATTIC, $\overline{\text{FINISH}}$, !TIRED!. ALL-EVENING,

$$\overline{\hspace{1cm}}^{t} \qquad \overline{\hspace{1cm}}^{t}$$

FRIEND CHILDREN, ME TAKING-CARE-OF. SUNDAY, ME TAKE-IT-

$$\overline{\hspace{1cm}}^{mm}$$

EASY, ALL-MORNING ME $\overline{\text{OVERSLEEP}}$, GET-UP, READING

$$\overline{\hspace{1cm}}^{t}$$

NEWSPAPER. ALL-AFTERNOON, FRIEND US-TWO GO-TO

$$\overline{\hspace{1cm}}^{when}$$

MUSIC/CONCERT, LISTENING, DANCING, FINISH, COME-TO

$$\overline{\hspace{1cm}}^{when}$$

HOME, STUDYING, $\overline{\text{FINISH}}$, GO-AWAY SLEEP.

A: OH-I-SEE...

VOCABULARY:

seasons	weekend activities	time signs
AUTUMN	seasonal tasks and activities	fs-WEEKEND
WINTER	events	WEEK+END
SPRING	short trips	#FS+SUNDAY
SUMMER		
YEAR-ROUND		

feelings about activities	opinions	feelings about disrupted plans	other
FEEL+GOOD	HARD	#UPSET	#BUSY
FEEL+"thumb up"	HELL	PISS+#OFF	IN-GEAR
SO-SO	NOT-CARE-FOR	FRUSTRATED	MESS-UP
BORED		DEPRESSED	FINISH TOUCH
BEAR-WITH	disruptions and disasters	MAD	FIRST-*thumb*+TIME
THRILLED	weather	BITTER	[(wh)5/IX-*mult*]
POOPED-OUT	health problems	DON'T-CARE	local sights
WORN-OUT	car problems	HAPPY, RELIEVED	and attractions
DIRTY "all over"	house problems	"snap fingers"	
fs-STIFF	personal reasons	"pshaw"	numbers:
	job-related reasons	DARN	120–1,000

SENTENCE STRUCTURES:

ask about the weekend

(time sign) [PAST] WEEK+END fs-WEEKEND PAST+#FS+SUNDAY	(person)	$\overline{\text{(2h)\#DO++}}^{\text{whq}}$ $\overline{\text{ENJOY}}^{\text{q}}$ $\overline{\text{"well"}}^{\text{q}}$ $\overline{\text{GOOD}}^{\text{q}}$

respond, describe activities over the weekend

(response) YES, [GOOD] SO-SO "well" #OK+ $\overline{\text{AWFUL}}^{\text{puff}}$	(time sign) PAST+FRIDAY PAST+SATURDAY PAST+SUNDAY	(part of day) ALL-MORNING ALL-AFTERNOON ALL-NIGHT ALL-DAY	(person)	(activity)	$\overline{\text{FINISH}}^{\text{when}}$	(next activity)	(feeling) (opinion) !TIRED! ENJOY	(repeat for next day of weekend)

GRAMMAR:

temporal sequencing: FINISH with when clause
time signs with durative aspect
element classifiers (Breakaway)

MATERIALS:

"Weekend Activities" worksheets 1 and 2
"Disrupted Plans" worksheet

blank cards

SIGN ILLUSTRATIONS:

YEAR-ROUND (see p. 152)
TAKE-IT-EASY (see p. 153)
DO-ERRANDS (see p. 153)
BEAR-WITH (see p. 153)
POOPED-OUT (see p. 154)
RENOVATE (see p. 155)
[(wh)5/IX-*mult*] (see p. 156)
NOT-CARE-FOR (see p. 156)
AMUSEMENT-PARK (see p. 157)
IN-GEAR (see p. 162)
BURN-DOWN (see p. 162)
BE-BEHIND-IN (see p. 163)
DARN (see p. 163)
POUR-MONEY-IN (see p. 164)
FIRST-*thumb* (see p. 166)

INTRODUCTION

Ask/Tell About Weekend Activities

1. Write the following list on the board:

> *What people do over the weekend during certain seasons:*
>
> - *usual activities*
> - *major tasks around the house*
> - *events*
> - *short trips*

Introduce the signs for seasons:

AUTUMN   **WINTER**   **SPRING**   **SUMMER**

For example, point to the word "seasons" on the board, spell the months in that season, then show the sign, i.e.:

> _____rhet____
> **T:** fs-SEPT, fs-OCT, fs-NOV, "what", AUTUMN.

Also introduce the sign **YEAR-ROUND**.

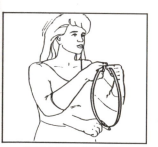

YEAR-ROUND

2. Usual Activities. Point on the board to "usual activities" and ask students what activities people usually do over a weekend in the fall:

> _____t_____whq___
> **T:** AUTUMN WEEK+END, PEOPLE TEND-TO ACT/DO "what".

Students should respond with signs they know, and act out or use gestures for other activities. Review or introduce the signs below, as well as signs for the activities that students suggest. (Do not write glosses on the board.)

autumn
WATCH FOOTBALL
RUNNING
SHOPPING NEW CLOTHES
STUDYING

Continue the same procedure for the other seasons, introducing the following signs:

TAKE-IT-EASY

winter
WATCH BASKETBALL
STAY HOME
READING
SEWING
KNITTING
[PLAY] PLAY-CARDS
PLAY GAME
ICE-SKATING

summer
CANNING
SWIMMING
WASH CAR
SUNBATHING
COOK fs-BBQ
WALKING (hiking)
TAKE-IT-EASY

year-round
EXERCISE
DO-ERRANDS
WATCH #TV
WASH-CLOTHES CLOTHES

DO-ERRANDS

spring
WASH CAR
WATCH BASEBALL
RUNNING
STUDYING
PLAY TENNIS

_____ mm
DRIVE IX-dir*"around"* (go for a drive)

3. Review vocabulary by asking students their opinions of each activity:

```
                    t _____ q
T: (activity sign), YOU LIKE (or ENJOY).
```

Draw a continuum on the board
to introduce or review the following
signs for students' responses:

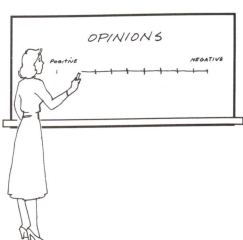

positive   negative
|___|___|___|___|___|___|___|___|___|
YES, ENJOY   YES, LIKE   YES, #FUN   #OK   SO-SO   #NO, BORED   #NO, BEAR-WITH   #NO, VOMIT

BEAR-WITH

Change the continuum on the board, then ask students how they usually feel after doing each activity:

when	whq

T: (activity sign) FINISH, HOW FEEL YOU.

Use the continuum to introduce or review these signs:

POOPED-OUT

refreshed   exhausted

FEEL+GOOD   HAPPY   RELIEVED   TIRED   POOPED-OUT   WORN-OUT
(or FEEL+"thumb up")

4. **Major Tasks.** Point to "major tasks around the house" on the board (see p. 152) and ask students what major tasks people might do over a weekend in the fall:

whq

T: (point to "major tasks around the house") AUTUMN "what".

Review old vocabulary (see especially Level 1, Unit 6) and introduce the following. (Do not write glosses on the board.)

autumn
LEAF RAKING
SWIMMING fs-POOL WATER (2h)DCL:B*"drain pool"*
fs-STORM WINDOW ICL*"put up"*

Continue the activity for the rest of the seasons, introducing the following signs:

winter
SNOW ICL*"shovel"*
TREE ICL*"prune"*
WOOD DCL*"logs"* ICL*"chop"*

summer
GRASS MOW
OUTSIDE PAINTING
fs-WEED ICL*"pull out"*
fs-FRUIT ICL*"pick from trees"*

spring
SOWING
SWIMMING fs-POOL WATER (2h)DCL:B*"fill up"*
fs-STORM WINDOW ICL*"take off"*
GARAGE CLEANING
PLANT DCL*"hedges"* ICL*"trim"*
MOVING*

year-round
PAINT SCRAPE-OFF
TO-PLASTER
PAINTING
BUILDING
FIX
(2h)#FIX++
HOUSE RENOVATE

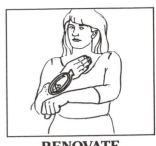

RENOVATE

5. Review vocabulary by asking students their opinions of the different tasks above. Introduce the signs **HARD** and **HELL**.

   Then ask students how they would feel after doing the tasks. Use the continuum and vocabulary lists above, and introduce additional vocabulary as follows:

   positive   negative

   |—————————————————|—————————————|—————————————|
   HAPPY FINISH   DIRTY "all over"   fs-STIFF   NEVER AGAIN

   Ask students what major household tasks they have done in the past. Have them describe how they felt while doing the task and after they finished it.

6. **Events.** Point on the board to "events" and ask students what special events people might attend on a weekend:

   ┌───┐
   │ _____t_____t_____whq   │
   │ **T:** DURING AUTUMN, WEEK+END, SPECIAL THRILL "what",   │
   │ _____whq   │
   │ PEOPLE TEND-TO PCL*"flock to"* "what".   │
   └───┘

---

*__NOTE:__ There are three related signs for the concept of "moving":
- MOVING (flat-O→spread-C++): the process of moving into another house, including packing and transporting things.
- MOVE-AWAY (flat-O→spread-C): to move away from one area to another, i.e., to a distant city or state, or move out of an area.
- MOVE-TO (flat-O): moving from one house to another, usually in the same area.

Repeat the same procedure for the rest of the seasons, introducing the vocabulary below:

autumn
HALLOWEEN PARTY
THANKSGIVING (2h)alt.EAT
DEAF KNOW WEEK (Deaf Awareness Week)

winter
CHRISTMAS PARTY
NEW YEAR PARTY

spring
WEDDING
fs-PROM
GRADUATE
EASTER
SPRING+VACATION
MEXICO CELEBRATE (Cinco de Mayo)

summer
WEDDING
PICNIC
MUSIC/CONCERT
VACATION
fs-JULY FOURTH

year-round
PARTY
PERFORMANCE
MEETING (conference)
WORKSHOP
PARADE
TOURNAMENT

Ask students which events they like the most and the least, and why (you may need to introduce the sign NOT-CARE-FOR):

[(wh)5/IX-*mult*]

NOT-CARE-FOR

T: WHICH [(wh)5/IX-*mult*] WEDDING, WORKSHOP, PARTY, MUSIC/CONCERT,
                           _____whq_____
 YOU LIKE BEST, WHICH.

S: (responds)

 _____whq_____
T: WHY LIKE, WHY.

S: (explains why)

                             _____whq_____
T: OH-I-SEE, WHICH YOU **NOT-CARE-FOR** WHICH.

S: (responds)

                     _____whq_____
T: WHY **NOT-CARE-FOR**, WHY.

S: (explains why)

Help students give reasons by introducing any necessary vocabulary and checking that their non-manual markers are appropriate for their feelings or opinions.

7. Short Trips. Point on the board to "short trips" and ask students what weekend trips people usually take:

            ____t____   ____whq____
T: WEEK+END, PEOPLE EXIT CITY GO-OUT, TEND-TO GO-OUT WHERE.

Review or introduce the following vocabulary. (Do not write glosses on the board.)

places to go
AMUSEMENT-PARK
GO-TO MOUNTAIN
GO-TO (city)
(names of local amusement parks or
    tourist attractions)

activities
GO-AROUND SIGHTSEEING
BOATING
WALKING (hiking)
CANOEING
FISHING
HUNTING
SKIING
fs-CC SKIING (cross country)
SLEDDING
MEETING (convention)
WORKSHOP

modes of transportation
FLY-TO
TAKE-TRAIN-TO
DRIVE-TO
fs-RENT CAR

where to stay
fs-MOTEL
fs-HOTEL
CAMPING
fs-CABIN

AMUSEMENT-PARK

Ask students where they would most like to go if:

• they had a weekend off
• they had a three-day holiday weekend in the summer
• they were taking their parents along
• they were going alone

For example:

		cond	
SUPPOSE	WEEK+END, REGULAR, SATURDAY+SUNDAY, YOU LOAF/RETIRE		WHERE YOU WANT _whq_
	!3-DAY! SATURDAY+SUNDAY+MONDAY, DURING SUMMER		
	YOUR MOTHER+FATHER PARTICIPATE-_you_ GO-OUT		GO-OUT, WHERE
	YOU GO-OUT ALONE		

Ask students to explain why they would choose each trip.

━━━━━━━━━━━━━━━━━━━━━━━━━ B R E A K A W A Y

GUESS THE OBJECT
(see Appendix, p. 170)

Purpose: To practice forming yes/no questions.

SIGN PRODUCTION

"Talking About Weekend Activities"

Purpose: To practice sequencing activities by using the sign FINISH in a when clause.

1. Write the following dialogue format on the board:

> **Signer A:** *ask about the weekend*
> **B:** *respond, describe your weekend activities*
> **A:** *comment*

Role play both Signers A and B, demonstrating how to ask about the weekend and how to describe activities. For example:

---

                                          q

A: WEEK+END ENJOY YOU.

                                          t

B: SO-SO, PAST+SATURDAY ALL-DAY ME STAY HOME, CLEANING, VACUUMING, WASH-CLOTHES CLOTHES, BOX PACKING, PUT-AWAY++

                     when

IX-loc*"up"* fs-ATTIC, **FINISH**, !TIRED!. ALL-EVENING,

                    t   t

FRIEND CHILDREN, ME TAKING-CARE-OF. SUNDAY, ME TAKE-IT-EASY,

                               mm

ALL-MORNING ME OVERSLEEP, GET-UP, READING NEWSPAPER.

                    t

ALL-AFTERNOON, FRIEND US-TWO GO-TO MUSIC/CONCERT, LISTENING,

         when   **when**

DANCING, **FINISH**, COME-TO HOME, STUDYING, **FINISH**, GO-AWAY SLEEP.

A: OH-I-SEE...

---

2. Review different phrases for asking about the weekend (line 1) using the following sentence structure:

ask about the weekend

(time sign)
[PAST] WEEK+END
fs-WEEKEND
PAST+#FS+SUNDAY
	(person)	whq
		(2h)#DO++
		     q
		ENJOY
		     q
		"well"
		     q
		GOOD

3. Demonstrate how to describe your weekend by telling a cluster of activities, then using FINISH in a when clause before telling the next cluster. Use the following sentence structure:

respond, describe activities over the weekend

(response) YES, [GOOD] SO-SO "well" #OK+ ___puff AWFUL	(time sign) PAST+FRIDAY PAST+SATURDAY PAST+SUNDAY	(part of day) ALL-MORNING ALL-AFTERNOON ALL-NIGHT ALL-DAY	(person)	(activity)	when FINISH	(next activity)	(feeling) (opinion) !TIRED! ENJOY	(repeat for next day of weekend)

4. Call two students up front to role play Signers A and B to talk about their weekend. Make sure they sequence activities and use the sign FINISH appropriately.*

5. Pair off students and hand out "Weekend Activities" Worksheet 1 to one student in each pair and "Weekend Activities" Worksheet 2 to the other (see Materials Appendix, pp. 175–176). Have students take turns being Signers A and B, following the dialogue format on the board.

■ B R E A K A W A Y

DESCRIBING ELEMENTS
(see Appendix, p. 170)

Purpose: To practice element classifiers (ECLs) for weather and different forms and intensities of gas, liquid, fire and light.

SIGN PRODUCTION

"Telling About Events and Short Trips"

Purpose: To practice descriptive vocabulary for telling about weekend activities and short trips.

1. Write the following dialogue format on the board:

---

*NOTE: Make sure students use appropriate phrasing for sequences of activities. After signing each cluster of activities, they should sign FINISH with a nod (and when-clause non-manual markers), then shift the body slightly to one side to sign the next activity or sequence.

Signer A: *ask about the weekend*
B: *comment, describe event or trip*

possible details

(1) *what the event/trip was for*
(2) *who attended/went along*
(3) *where it occurred*
(4) *what the environment was like*
(5) *what people wore (clothing, make-up,*
    hairstyles, etc.)
(6) *what you and others did*
(7) *what happened*
(8) *give opinions*

A: *comment or ask for more information*

Role play both Signers A and B in a sample dialogue about an actual event or short trip. For example, tell about a wedding you attended:

<u>   q   </u>
A: PAST WEEK+END YOU ENJOY.
B: !ENJOY! PAST+SATURDAY ME GO-TO WEDDING, NICE, BEAUTIFUL,
<u>   q   </u>
!DIFFERENT!. YOU KNOW L-*on-chest*(Laura). THAT-ONE IX MARRIED
MAN, HEARING. WEDDING POSS MOTHER+FATHER HOME OUTSIDE
BACK fs-YARD. NICE DECORATE, CHAIR DCL*"chairs arranged in a semi-*
circle", PEOPLE PCL*"look at center"*; BRIDESMAID, MAN (2h)SCL:1*"enter*
from the side and meet at the center" L-*on-chest*, POSS MOTHER+FATHER
SCL:3*"enter and join the wedding party"*. . . (add other details)
<u>   whq   </u>
A: WHERE GO-OUT HONEYMOON, WHERE.

---

2. Point to (1) on the board, "what the event/trip was for," and ask students to answer based on your narrative. Go through the rest of the list and have students repeat the details you gave. Then call two students up front to practice the dialogue.

3. Ask a student to describe an event s/he participated in. Then go through the list of possible details and ask about each one. From the student's answers, help him/her select appropriate details for the narrative. Also help the student with appropriate vocabulary choices and an opening and closing for the narrative.

Then have the student repeat the narrative according to your feedback.

4. Demonstrate another sample dialogue, this time about a short trip (for example, to Hearst Castle):

$$\overline{\hspace{4cm}}^{q}$$

A: PAST WEEK+END "well".

$$\overline{\hspace{0.8cm}}^{nod}$$

B: GOOD. PAST+#FS+SUNDAY US-THREE GO-OUT fs-SLO (San Luis Obispo), ENJOY SIGHTSEEING, GO-TO PLAY fs-BEACH, GO-TO VISIT fs-HEARST

$$\overline{\hspace{2cm}}^{t/q}$$

fs-CASTLE, YOU KNOW !FAMOUS! SCL:claw*"mansion on a hill"* HOME !(2h)alt.FANCY!. REAL/TRUE BEAUTIFUL. ME BE-ATTRACTED SWIMMING fs-POOL. !WOW! FACE+SAME-AS POSS GREECE. STATUE STAND (2h)SCL:A*"statues encircling the pool"*, DCL*"columns"* (2h)SCL:1*"columns around the pool"*. . .

$$\overline{\hspace{4cm}}^{q}$$

A: "wow" ME WANT GO-TO SEE. EXPENSIVE ENTER.

---

5. Again point to (1) on the board, "what the event/trip was for," and ask students to answer based on your narrative. Go through the rest of the list and have students repeat whatever details you gave.

6. Call on other students to briefly describe a recent trip, workshop, retreat, concert or performance. Go through the list again and help students select details as above. Also give feedback on openings and closings, then have them repeat the narratives.

7. Pair up students and have them practice narratives about events they attended or their own recent short trips. Encourage students to use the list on the board to help each other select details.

   Afterwards call a few students up front to tell their narratives to the whole class. Give feedback on:

   - vocabulary choices
   - amount and kinds of detail
   - narrative opening and closing

■ BREAKAWAY

NUMBERS

Introduce numbers 120 – 1,000

First practice multiples of 100 to 1,000.

Then practice the rest of the numbers by signing a number and asking students to give you the number that precedes or follows it, i.e.:

$$\overline{\hspace{0.5cm}}^{t}\overline{\hspace{1.5cm}}^{cs}\overline{\hspace{1cm}}^{whq}$$

T: 125, NEXT-TO "what".
S: 126.

Vary the activity by signing a number and having students add 10 or 100 to it, then tell you the new number, i.e.:

$$\overline{\hspace{1.5cm}}^{whq}$$

T: 450 PLUS 100 "what".
S: 550.

INTRODUCTION

Telling How Plans Have Been Disrupted

1. Write the following list on the board:

Weekend plans disrupted because of:

- *weather*
- *health problems*
- *house problems*
- *car problems*
- *personal reasons*
- *job-related reasons*

Ask students what things (both everyday occurrences and disasters) might disrupt people's plans for the weekend:

$$\overline{\hspace{6cm}}^{\text{t}}$$
T: YOU KNOW++ WEEK+END PLAN IN-GEAR, SOMETIMES MESS-UP,
$$\underline{\hspace{2cm}}_{\text{stress}} \quad \overline{\hspace{1.5cm}}^{\text{whq}}$$
fs-OR AWFUL HAPPEN, WHY.

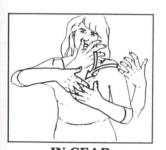

IN-GEAR

Point to each category on the board and introduce or review the following vocabulary. (Do not write glosses on the board.) Add other related vocabulary as necessary.

weather
RAIN (various degrees)
SNOW (various degrees) } (see Appendix, pp. 170–174)
WINDY (various degrees)
LOUSY fs-WEATHER
fs-FOG
fs-HURRICANE
TORNADO

health problems
SICK
EMERGENCY
BRING-TO HOSPITAL

house problems
WATER+DCL"*flood*"
WATER+ECL:4"*leak*"
HOUSE BURN-DOWN
ELECTRIC+ECL"*black out*"
HOUSE BREAK+ENTER

BURN-DOWN

car problems
[CAR] BREAKDOWN
CAR-ACCIDENT
CAR STEAL
fs-BATTERY (or ELECTRIC) DEAD
WINDOW CRACKED
TIRE DCL"flat"
WATER ECL:5wg"steam" ECL:S→5"water gushes out of radiator"

personal reasons
BE-LOST TICKET (MONEY, KEYS)
VERBAL-FIGHT
BREAK+#UP
FRIEND DROP [PLAN], ME STUCK
MOTHER+FATHER (or FRIEND) APPEAR, SURPRISE

job-related reasons
BE-BEHIND-IN WORK
WORKSHOP
MEETING
#OT (overtime)
LAID-OFF
FIRED

BE-BEHIND-IN

2. Ask students how they feel when their plans are disrupted:

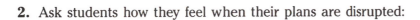

	t	th		whq
T: WEEK+END PLAN, MESS-UP, HOW FEEL YOU.				

Draw a continuum on the board
and introduce the following
reaction vocabulary:

negative   positive

MAD   DEPRESSED   DARN   DON'T CARE HAPPY, RELIEVED
PISS+#OFF   FRUSTRATED   "snap fingers"
#UPSET   BITTER   "pshaw"

DARN

SIGN PRODUCTION

"And Then the Water Pipes Burst . . . "

Purpose: To practice telling about disrupted plans.

1. Write the following dialogue format on the board:

> ***Signer A:*** *ask about the weekend*
>   ***B:*** *complain*
>   ***A:*** *respond, ask what happened*
>   ***B:*** *tell about disrupted plans, including how you felt*
>   ***A:*** *respond*

2. Hand out the "Disrupted Plans" worksheets (see Materials Appendix, p. 177). Role play both Signers A and B in a dialogue based on the Sample Situation. For example:

>   t   q
> **A:** PAST WEEK+END, GOOD.
>
> **B:** "pshaw" AWFUL, LOUSY.
>   whq
> **A:** WHAT'S-MATTER.
>
> **B:** !RAIN-*cont*! SICK-OF. FRIEND US-TWO GO-OUT CAMPING IX-loc MOUNTAIN.
>   when   puff cheeks
> ARRIVE, **WRONG** RAIN ICL*"pour bucketsful"*. CAMPING "area" !WET!
> WATER+ECL*"flooded"*. CAN'T CAMPING. US-TWO LOOK-FOR FIND
> fs-MOTEL. RAIN-*cont* STAY-*cont* #FS+SUNDAY. MONEY POUR-MONEY-IN.
> NONE OUTSIDE PLAY, COOK, EAT, !NONE!. ME BITTER.
>   stress
> **A:** AWFUL, PITY-*you*.

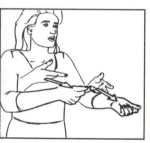

POUR-MONEY-IN

Call on students to role play Signers A and B in a dialogue about the same situation.

3. Have students read Situation 1. Introduce key signs for the situation:

WINDY (vary intensity)
PAPER DCL*"plates and cups"*
LCL:C*"cups being blown away"*

Then call up two students to role play Signers A and B.

4. Continue with the other situations. Key signs for each one are listed below. Encourage students to use the sign WRONG with appropriate phrasing.

Situation 2: STING   DCL*"swollen"*
                 CAN'T BREATHE   BRING-TO HOSPITAL

Situation 3: DCL*"dead bolt"* BROKE   #ALL WINDOW LOCKED
                 KEY ICL*"insert key in lock"*

Situation 4: WARN LIGHT ECL*"light comes on"*
                 SMELL fs-BURN
                 WATER ECL:5wg*"steam"*
                 WATER ECL:S→5*"water gushes out of radiator"*
                 TOW

Situation 5: PHONE DISCONNECT
                 MOTHER+FATHER APPEAR, SURPRISE

Situation 6: WEEK+END LOAF/RETIRE
                 OTHER WORK+ER SICK
                 #OT (overtime)

5. Divide the class into pairs. Have students go through the dialogue format for each situation on the worksheet. They should explain how their weekend plans were disrupted, reviewing phrases introduced above.

6. Ask students if they've experienced disrupted weekend plans. Call several students up front to describe their experiences.

INTRODUCTION

Telling What Sights to See

1. Tell students that a guest from out of town will visit them this weekend. The guest will want to know what places s/he should visit in the area. Ask students what places they would recommend. List the suggestions on the board, and introduce signs (if any) for the places.

For example, for the San Francisco Bay Area:

Write on board:	Introduce signs:
San Francisco	#SF
Chinatown	CHINA+TOWN
Great America	LARGE AMERICA
S.F. Zoo	fs-ZOO
Golden Gate Bridge	fs-GG BRIDGE
Golden Gate Park	fs-GG fs-PARK
cable cars	fs-CABLE fs-CAR
Alcatraz	fs-ALCATRAZ ISLAND
Marine World	fs-MARINE WORLD
Napa Valley	fs-NAPA WINE "area"

2. Ask students about each place:

   • what there is to see or do
   • what they think of it
   • how much it costs
   • if it is a good place for children
   • if it is accessible (flat terrain, barrier-free, close to transportation)

3. Ask students which places they would suggest if the guest:

   • has a whole week to visit
   • has only one night and one day to visit
   • has only five hours to visit
   • has a car
   • is on foot

Be sure students use sequencing (or listing) when telling which places to see, i.e.:

MUST SEE FIRST-*thumb* fs-GG BRIDGE, IX-*index* CHINA+TOWN, IX-*middle* fs-CABLE fs-CAR RIDE.

FIRST-*thumb*

SIGN PRODUCTION

"Recommending Places to Visit"

Purpose: To review vocabulary and phrases, and develop fluency and turn-taking skills.

1. Write the following dialogue format on the board:

Situation: *Signer A is going to a big city for the weekend. Signer B has been there before and recommends a few places to visit.*

line 1	**A:**	*ask if B has ever been to a certain big city*
2	**B:**	*reply affirmatively, tell how long ago or how many times*
3	**A:**	*respond, tell B you will go there in two weeks, and tell how you feel about it*
4	**B:**	*ask if it is A's first time there*
5	**A:**	*reply affirmatively, ask B to recommend places to visit*
6	**B:**	*find out what A is interested in*
7	**A:**	*tell B what you like to do*
8	**B:**	*recommend three places*
9	**A:**	*clarify some details about each place*
10	**B:**	*respond*

Role play both Signers A and B in the following sample dialogue:

                                                              _____q___
line 1 **A:** FINISH TOUCH NEW-YORK BEFORE, YOU.

  2 **B:** YES, ME GO-TO++ 2, 3 TIME.

  3 **A:** !FINE!. ME PLAN GO-TO NEW-YORK TWO-WEEKS-FUTURE. ME
           EXCITED.
                                                         _____q___
  4 **B:** !REAL/TRUE! YOUR FIRST-*thumb*+TIME GO-TO.
                           ___nod___   _____whq___
  5 **A:** YES, FIRST-*thumb*+TIME. ME SHOULD SEE "what".
                                    ____whq___
           NEW-YORK POSS THRILL "what".
                                    _____
  6 **B:** !MANY! DIFFERENT++. YOU LIKE GO-OUT EAT,
                                    _____q___
           SHOPPING, SIGHTSEEING, YOU.

  7 **A:** ME WANT SIGHTSEEING ENJOY, LEARN++.
                                              _____
  8 **B:** FINE++. MAYBE YOU ENJOY GO-TO BOAT SEE, KNOW
                           ____t___
           WOMAN BCL"*Statue of Liberty*", CAN ENTER SCL:V"*walk
           up stairs*" IX-loc"*go up to top*". OTHER IX-*index*, IX-loc"*go up*"
           fs-EMPIRE fs-STATE BUILDING. IX-*middle* YOU SHOULD GO-TO
           fs-GV(Greenwich Village). !INTERESTING!. NEW-YORK SWELL
           fs-SUBWAY IX-dir"*go everywhere*" FAST.
           _____
  9 **A:** WOMAN BCL"*Statue of Liberty*" ENTER, PLUS BOAT
                           ___t___   _____whq___
           ALL-TOGETHER, COST HOW-MUCH.

  10 **B:** NOT+SURE. MAYBE FIVE-DOLLARS, SIX-DOLLARS.

2. Call two students up front to role play the dialogue. Suggest that they think of
another city that Signer B has actually been to.

3. Divide the class into pairs. Have students write down the cities they've been to so
that their partners know what city to ask about. Have each pair exchange lists,
then practice the dialogue.

4. After pair practice, have the whole class discuss the best sights to see in
various cities. Encourage students to agree or disagree with others' comments
and suggestions.

INTERACTION

A Weekend to Remember

Purpose: To review vocabulary and phrases for activities, events, short trips and money while making weekend plans.

1. Tell the class to develop a list of activities for a special weekend for the whole class.

2. Divide the class into groups of four or five students each. Tell each group they have up to 40 minutes to develop plans for an ideal weekend.

   Write on the board:

   > *Consider these:*
   >
   > - *activities (include time, length of activity, places to go)*
   > - *meals*
   > - *transportation*
   > - *expenses*
   > - *any special considerations, i.e., interpreter, elevators, break times*
   > - *equipment (i.e., maps, flashlight, tents)*
   > - *kind of clothes to wear*
   > - *souvenirs available*
   > - *meetings with celebrities*
   > - *emergency plans*
   > *etc.*

3. When time is up, have each group present its plan to the class. One student should facilitate the group's presentation; others in the group should each give information about different parts of their plan.

4. When all groups' plans are shared, have the whole class vote on which plan they would choose. Tally the votes. If time permits, discuss reasons why certain plans were popular and others less popular.

   Variation: Instead of planning something for the whole class, have each group plan weekend activities for one of the following groups of people:

   - group of Deaf adults from the local area
   - group of senior citizens from your area
   - group of visitors from out of state or from another country
   - group of jocks (i.e., football team from a distant university)
   - group of rich people
   - group of nature lovers
   - Boy Scout troop on a camping trip

   When time is up, have each group share its plan with the rest of the class. Give feedback on their signing and encourage the class to give feedback on the ideas.

STUDENT VIDEOTEXT AND WORKBOOK

1. Make sure students complete the video-interactive and other activities for this unit, either in class or for homework. Also assign the Culture/Language Notes for this unit.

End of Unit 17

APPENDIX

GUESS THE OBJECT

1. Write each of the following words on index cards or slips of paper (or find pictures of each object). Tape one card to the back of each student *without* showing the student the word or picture on the card.

size AA battery	snorkle
bicycle horn	flippers
parking meter	scooter
mirror	baseball mitt
mailbox	pompom
contact lenses	diamond ring
folding fan	baby pacifier
conch shell	compass
light bulb	avocado
snowshoe	walking cane

2. This game is a version of "Twenty Questions." Each student is to guess the object on his/her card by asking other students yes/no questions until s/he guesses the object correctly.

   Encourage students to walk around the room and mingle with each other. Students may look at the cards taped to other students' backs, but not at the cards on their own backs. Make sure they ask yes/no questions; answers should be either yes or no.

DESCRIBING ELEMENTS

Descriptive classifiers (DCLs) describe things that have specific shapes and sizes. **Element classifiers** (ECLs), however, often describe things that do not have specific shapes or sizes, and are in constant motion, i.e., weather, or elements such as water, air, fire, light.

1. Begin by introducing the following vocabulary:

   fs-AIR
   WINDY
   WATER
   RAIN
   SNOW
   FIRE
   LIGHT (illumination)

Then demonstrate how you can vary descriptions of each element by using classifiers:

air
air blowing out, i.e., exhaust from tailpipe
air being sucked in, i.e., vacuum
smoke-filled room
vapors from an open freezer

wind
light breeze
strong but brief gust from one direction
winds in a bad storm

water
a small brook
water from hose at full blast
ocean waves

light
alternating flashing red lights at a railroad crossing
flash from a camera
light from a lighthouse

rain
light drizzle
hard rain
ordinary but steady rain

snow
flurries
ordinary but steady snow
heavy snow (blizzard)

fire
fire in a fireplace
flame on a candle
torch flame
forest fire

2. Ask students questions such as:

   • what does it look like when... (see list below)
   • what happens when... (see list below)

Encourage students to come up with element classifiers on their own. Afterwards, demonstrate the correct form of the following element classifier signs.

Air/Wind/Smoke

(2h)ECL:5
   • standing 50 feet from a helicopter about to land
   • standing on a cliff by the ocean
   • riding downhill on a bicycle
   • walking on a fine breezy day
   • the fog drifting over the San Francisco Bay
   • air circulating around room
   • heat shimmering in air (i.e., above a road)

ECL:S→5 "blowing out"
   • holding a blow dryer in front of your face
   • someone blowing cigarette smoke in your face
   • blowing out cigarette smoke
   • a bull snorting

ECL:spread-C
- vacuum sucking air/dirt in
- dentist's tool sucking water from mouth
- smoke drifting from a cigarette
- odor from armpits
- smoke from recently extinguished candle
- smoke from recently fired pistol

Water/Rain/Snow

ECL:S→1
- a coffee pot percolating
- a dripping faucet
- a person spitting as s/he talks
- a few drops of rain (at beginning or end of storm)
- a small trickle of water from a garden hose

(2h)ECL:S→5
- small splash when a pebble is thrown in water
- big splash from a person diving into water
- water gushing out of an overheated radiator (one hand)
- splash from a cup of water thrown at you
- spills: fallen glass, dropped bucket

ECL:4
- a running faucet
- water coming out of the drain hole in a cooler
- an infant drooling
- blood pouring out of a cut

(2h)ECL:5wg
- Niagara Falls
- a torrential river or rapids
- a meandering stream
- ocean waves pounding the shore on a stormy day
- high ocean waves perfect for surfing
- waves created by a passing boat on a lake
- steady snow to blizzard
- overflowing container, i.e, sink, tub, pitcher (one hand)

(2h)ECL:claw
- rain (from ordinary to hard rain)

ECL:spread-C
- water being flushed down a toilet
- water gushing continually out of a firefighter's hose

(2h)ECL/DCL:L*"spreading"*
- growing spot of liquid on a surface
- ripples in water after a splash

Fire

(2h)ECL:5wg
- a roaring fire in a fireplace
- gas flame for low heat
- gas flame for medium heat
- a bonfire
- a forest fire

ECL:5wg
- a candle flame

ECL:S→5wg

- fire quickly consuming a forest
- fire moving up your sleeve
- a dragon breathing fire

Light

ECL:flat-O→spread-C
- headlights of a car
- brake lights
- flashing hazard lights
- traffic lights
- dawn/dusk (getting dimmer or brighter)
- lights flashing across a computer screen
- twinkling lights (Christmas tree lights or stars)
- light from a flash bulb

ECL:spread-C
- siren lights
- spotlight, desk light, flashlight
- dimmed lights
- bright lights
- lights flickering when the power is about to go out

ECL:1(zig zag)
- a flash of lightning

ECL:S→1
- a laser beam

3. Divide the class into groups of four, and have them work together to develop a story using different element classifiers. Then have each person in a group tell different parts of the story. For example:

There was a tall building on fire; the fire was moving up its walls. Siren lights were flashing, a fire truck pulled in. Someone grabbed a hose, turned it on, and water burst out. The building collapsed, and smoke rose from the rubble.

Sample story:

S1: BUILDING LCL:B*"tall rectangle"*. FIRE ECL:5*"up the walls"*.

S2: ECL:5*"flashing lights"* SCL:3*"car pulls in"*.

S3: ICL*"hold hose"* ICL*"pull down lever"* WATER ECL*"gushes out"*.

S4: BUILDING (2h)LCL:5*"collapses"* ECL:5*"smoke swirling around"*.

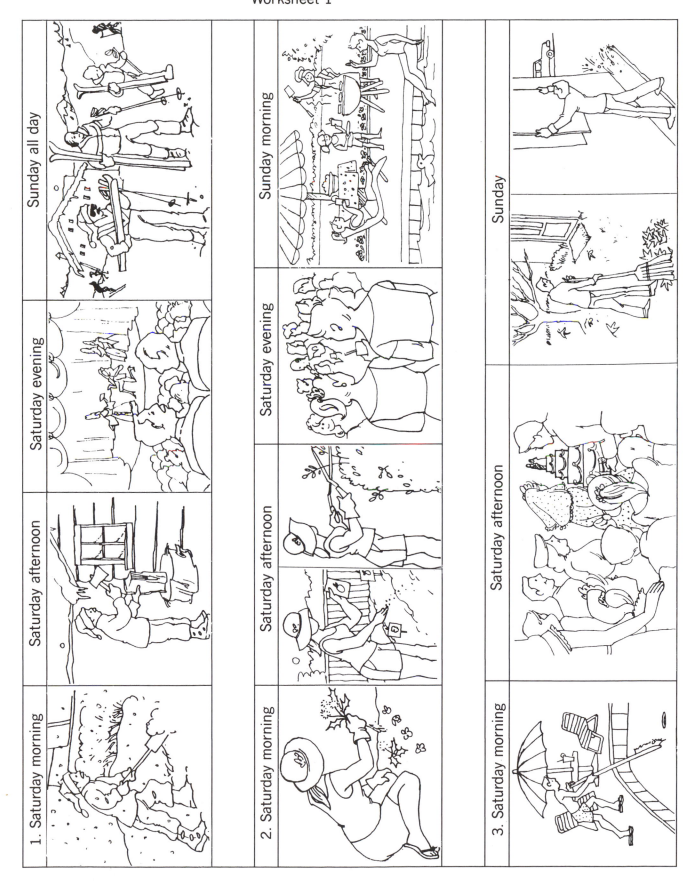

WEEKEND ACTIVITIES
(for p. 159)

Worksheet 2

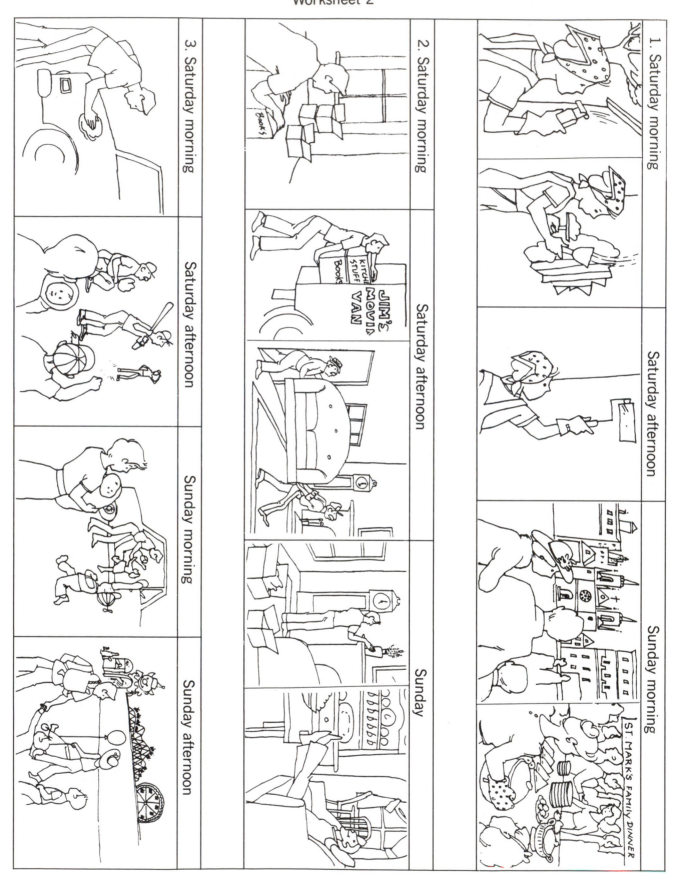

"DISRUPTED PLANS"
(for p. 164)
Worksheet

Sample Situation: You and a friend went camping in the mountains. When you arrived it was raining cats and dogs, and the campground was flooded. You ended up in a motel room, spending more money and missing all the fun of camping.

Situation 1: You planned a birthday party for your daughter at the park. When you arrived in the morning there was a gentle breeze. By the time you were ready to sing "Happy Birthday," the wind was blowing hard. Plates went flying, cups tipped over. Children were complaining. You had to pack up the food and the kids and go home.

Situation 2: A group of you went to the beach for the day. You spent the morning playing volleyball. At lunch a friend leaned over to reach for the punch and a bee stung her forearm repeatedly. Her arm immediately started to swell and she became short of breath. You rushed her to the hospital.

Situation 3: You arrived home to change clothes to attend your mother and father's 25th wedding anniversary that night. When you tried to unlock the door you realized your lock was broken. There was no open window. You had to call your landlord to fix the lock. You ended up going to the store to buy clothes for the party. You arrived late.

Situation 4: Sunday morning you packed up and took off for the lake. By mistake you took a wrong turn and ended up taking the long way. The road was windy and narrow so you couldn't turn around. You smelled something burning and the red warning light came on. Steam was coming out from under the hood. You reached the top of the hill where there was a small general store and gas station. You pulled over and opened your hood to find water gushing from the radiator. The gas station didn't have the parts you needed. You had to wait for a tow truck to take you home.

Situation 5: You and your husband were looking forward to spending the weekend alone. The kids were spending the night with friends. You disconnected the phone, and were just about to sit down to a candlelight dinner when the doorbell rang. It was your parents paying you a surprise visit from out of state.

Situation 6: You had the weekend off work and planned to stay overnight at the Renaissance Faire. Saturday morning you got up early, packed the car and had your coffee. Just as you were about to lock the door, the phone rang and you went back to answer it. It was your boss calling to tell you she needed you to come in because another employee was sick.

UNITS 13–17
CUMULATIVE REVIEW
O V E R V I E W

FOCUS:

Students are exposed to Deaf cultural behaviors, values and norms, including how to get and direct attention, how to resume a conversation, and how to control the pace of conversation. In role-play situations, they practice sharing relevant information to make connections between people and promote continuity.

VIDEOTAPED DIALOGUES:

In *Dialogue 7*, a Deaf woman preparing for a trip explains dog care and household duties to her hearing housesitter. The dialogue shows appropriate response behaviors and how signers control the pace of conversation.

In *Dialogue 8*, two women exchange information about a Deaf man (appearance, family information, community involvement), in order to understand how he is connected to the Deaf community. The dialogue also shows how the signer resumes the topic of conversation after a digression.

In *Dialogue 9*, three people discuss one man's family background and noticeable family traits. They demonstrate a culturally appropriate way of discussing deafness in a family. The dialogue also shows techniques of group conversation: eye gaze, interrupting, and directing attention.

NARRATIVES:

In the first narrative, "Lost Keys," Lee Ann Poynor describes her search for a lost set of keys. In the second narrative, "My Family Roots," Ken Pedersen talks about his ancestry and his sister's trip to Europe to visit their ancestors' birthplaces and family burial sites.

VOCABULARY AND PHRASES:

ANYWAY, THAT-ONE...
$$\overline{\hspace{3cm}}^{\text{whq}}$$
JUST-NOW ME SAY #WHAT

ANYWAY, ME [OFF-POINT] BACK-TO-POINT
 [THAT-ONE]...
$$\overline{\hspace{2cm}}^{\text{q}}$$
REAL/TRUE
$$\overline{\hspace{1cm}}^{\text{q}}$$
RIGHT
$$\overline{\hspace{1cm}}^{\text{q}}$$
QMwg

GRAMMAR:

confirming questions
locative classifiers
descriptive classifiers
instrument classifiers

MATERIALS:

Cumulative Review Level 2 videotape
"Comprehension Questions for Dialogue 8"
  transparency
"Whose Turn Is It?" instruction cards
"Conversation Strategies" transparency
"Is That So?" transparencies
"Making Connections" transparency
"My Family Roots" transparency
"Map of Canada" transparency
"The Lost Ring" activity sheet

decks of cards, Dominoes or other games
pictures of comic-strip characters and
  brand-name products
blank cards

IN PREPARATION

This unit is based on Dialogues 7–9 and the first two narratives in the *Cumulative Review Level 2* videotape. Preview the dialogues to familiarize yourself with the functions expressed and the cultural behaviors shown. Be sure to read the instructions for introducing each dialogue so you can prepare the activities beforehand. Preview the narratives as well, following Dialogue 9.

COMPREHENSION

Videotaped Dialogues

Dialogue 7

1. Show the videotape of Dialogue 7. Explain any signs or phrases that students do not understand.

   Then show the dialogue again and tell students to pretend that they are the housesitter hired by the Deaf person in the video. Have students make a list of things they need to do while the owner is away.

2. Have students tell you the different tasks they wrote down on their lists.

Dialogue 8

3. Show *part* of the videotape of Dialogue 8. Stop the tape a minute and eight seconds from the beginning of the dialogue, right after Cinnie says:

   SWELL !SICK-YOU! US-TWO AVOID-EACH-OTHER. NOT-KNOW US-TWO DEAF, !SICK-YOU! "pshaw". . .

   Explain to students how the man in the story found out Cinnie is Deaf, and why Cinnie felt silly after realizing the man is Deaf.

4. Continue showing the rest of Dialogue 8.

   Point out how Cinnie tried to describe and identify the man she met, and how later she and Mary tried to figure out his affiliations with the Deaf community.

5. Show the "Comprehension Questions for Dialogue 8" transparency (see Materials Appendix, p. 199). Show the dialogue again if necessary and explain any signs or phrases that students do not understand.

   Have students answer the questions in sign. (The answers are provided below for the teacher's reference.)

Answers to Comprehension Questions for Dialogue 8

1) There was a long line at the snack bar, and she was talking with a Deaf man she met in line.

2) Cinnie complains that it's overcast and thinks it may rain. Mary doesn't think it will rain.

3) Cinnie gestured to the snack bar worker that she is Deaf, and asked for pen and paper to order food.

4) Silly, because she should have known the man was Deaf. She sensed something about him, but didn't follow her intuition.

5) Nick Oren. They attended Gallaudet College at the same time, but he was a few years ahead of Mary.

6) Supervisor at IBM.

7) Four children. The first three are Deaf.

8) The oldest resembles the father; the second and third look like both parents; the last one resembles the mother.

9) Nick is vice-president of the California Association of the Deaf.

Dialogue 9

6. Before showing the videotape of Dialogue 9, write on the board:

> *In Dialogue 9, Dennis Waterhouse talks about his surname, his ancestry, and possible causes of his deafness.*
>
> *Look for the following:*
>
> - *family's original name*
> - *nationality*
> - *genetic trait in his family*
> - *three possible causes of his deafness*
> - *how his daughter's hearing was tested*

7. Show the dialogue. Explain any signs or phrases that students do not understand.

Then ask the following **comprehension questions** and have students answer the questions in sign. Refer to the list on the board and ask:

- What was Dennis's family's original name? (*Answer*: Wasserhaus; surname changed when family moved to America)

- What was Dennis's nationality? (*Answer*: German)

- What genetic trait appears around age 30? (*Answer*: among relatives on his mother's side, hair color changes to white)

- What were the three opinions given by doctors about the cause of Dennis's deafness? (*Answer*: 1) he was a breech baby;* 2) damage from forceps as doctor rushed to deliver him because of lack of oxygen; 3) genetic reasons: a certain gene related to deafness was passed down to Dennis)

- How was Dennis's daughter's hearing tested? (*Answer*: first by making noise behind her to see if she would respond, then by having an EEG measure electrical impulses)

Additional questions:

- Did Dennis have any other ancestors or relatives who were also deaf? (*Answer*: none — Dennis is the first one)

- Why did the hearing woman interrupt Dennis (*Answer*: because Dennis had only ten minutes left on his parking meter)

DISCUSSION

Cultural Behaviors and Conversation Strategies

1. Write on the board:

> *Look for:*
>
> - *how people get or direct attention*
> - *how people respond to information*
> - *how people resume the topic of conversation*
> - *how people keep each other informed*

Dialogue 7

2. Show Dialogue 7 again, this time having students focus on the things listed above. Then discuss the following:

Getting/directing attention

Darah **signs "wait a sec"** to Mary to indicate she is not ready to resume conversation (so she can make a list).

Darah **waves in** Mary's **peripheral vision** while Mary looks away or is thinking.

---

*NOTE: UCCD is an acronym for the University of California Center on Deafness in San Francisco, a center for mental health research and clinical services for deaf people and their families.

Responding to information

$$\overline{q}$$
Darah repeats ICL*"pull"*.
Darah repeats TWICE+WEEK.

Keeping each other informed

Mary cautions Darah about one neighbor's dislike of dogs peeing on her lawn.

Dialogue 8

3. Show Dialogue 8 again. Observe and discuss the following:

Getting/directing attention

Cinnie approaches Mary at the table and **taps her elbow**.

Responding to information

Cinnie signs the phrases:

> ALL-RIGHT THAT-ONE (about Nick Oren)
> OH-I-SEE
> OF-COURSE (to Deaf parents)
> $\overline{q}$
> REAL/TRUE (about supervisor at IBM)
> "oh" YES (to CAD clarification)

Mary signs the phrase: !THAT-ONE!

Cinnie signs the phrases:

> SMALL WORLD INTERESTING
> IX*"related"* AUNT (nod)

Resuming previous topic of conversation

Cinnie repeats the last phrase she signed before going off the topic:

$$\overline{}\text{neg/q}$$
Cinnie: **AWFUL !PCL:4*"long line"*!** fs-WEATHER ECL*"overcast sky"* RAIN QMwg.

$$\overline{}\text{neg}\qquad\overline{}\text{q}$$
Mary: FACE+SAME-AS. BE-SKEPTICAL. #OK COLD YOU.

Cinnie: #OK "pshaw" FINE, REAL/TRUE **AWFUL PCL:4*"long line"*.** . .

Keeping each other informed

a) about what happened, for example:
   Cinnie explains to Mary about her meeting Nick in the food line.

b) about a person's background (making connections between people), for example:

Mary thinks of various ways Cinnie can get the connection to Nick.

c) about distracting things in a person's appearance, for example:

Mary tells Cinnie about food on her cheek.

Dialogue 9

4. Show Dialogue 9 again. Observe and discuss the following:

Getting/directing attention

Ella **taps** Carlene's **arm with the back of her hand** while Carlene was watching Dennis, then interrupts and adds information.

Ella directs Carlene's attention to Dennis by **leaning slightly towards him with intense eye gaze**, indicating that she should look at him (just before Dennis talks about his daughter).

Ella directs Carlene's attention to Dennis by **pointing to Dennis** when Carlene was looking at Ella and Dennis began to sign.

Responding to information

Carlene signs the phrases:
        SICK-YOU SWELL (to WATER+HOUSE)
        (shake head, repeats Ella's signs RED+HAIR)
        OH-I-SEE, JAW-DROP
        <u>   q   </u>
        FIRST (repeating that Dennis is the first Deaf person in his family)

Carlene and Ella sign: OH-I-SEE; INTERESTING
Dennis signs: RIGHT, THAT-ONE, EXACT

Resuming previous topic of conversation

Dennis asks others to help him remember where he left off:
                                                            whq
Dennis: **"what" ME SAY JUST-NOW, "what" ME SAY.**
Carlene: "well" YOU NARRATE HOW BECOME DEAF, [(wh)3/IX-*mult*]. . .
Ella: "hey" [(wh)3/IX-*index*], fs-FORCEPS, IX*"direct attention to Dennis"*
Carlene: (nod) ICL*"forceps on head"*
Dennis: RIGHT++, REMEMBER, THAT-ONE, THAT+TIME. . .

Keeping each other informed

a) about a person's background (making connections between people), for example:

Ella explains to Carlene what she knows about Dennis's boyhood

b) about new information, for example:

Ella explains to Carlene the latest technology for testing an infant's hearing.

INTRODUCTION

Directing and Maintaining Attention

1. Write on the board:

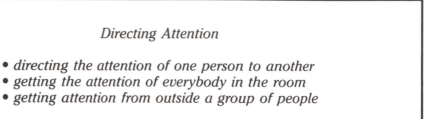

> *Directing Attention*
>
> • *directing the attention of one person to another*
> • *getting the attention of everybody in the room*
> • *getting attention from outside a group of people*

Directing attention of one person to another

2. Call two students to sit at a table up front to role play Signers A and B while you role play Signer C (see drawing for positioning each person).

Have Signer A start to sign to you while Signer B is either looking down or looking at you. Demonstrate each method listed below to direct Signer B's attention to Signer A:

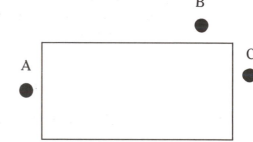

• tap person and point
• tap table and point
• lean toward speaker, point
• give name or name sign and point

Call up other students to role play Signer C and practice directing attention.

Getting the attention of everybody in the room

3. Demonstrate how to get the attention of everybody in the room by *waving with both hands and glancing all around to make sure everybody has their eyes on you.*

Hand out a different "Whose Turn Is It?" instruction card to each student (see Materials Appendix, pp. 200–201). Each card is part of a sequence of instructions.

Explain the rules:

a) Whoever has the turn must get everybody's attention.

b) If you can't get a person's attention, tell someone nearby to tap the person's shoulder and direct his/her attention to the signer.

c) The signer must check around and make sure s/he has everyone's attention before proceeding with the instructions on his/her card.

Make sure students mill around the room so that they don't know when it's their turn until they see their cue.

Getting attention from outside a group of people

4. Show the *top* half of the "Conversation Strategies" transparency (Getting Attention) or make copies of it and hand them out to students (see Materials Appendix, p. 202).

   Call five students up front to sit around a table. Give them a deck of cards and have them play a game (i.e., Gin, Hearts, Fish, Uno; or bring a set of Dominoes).

   Demonstrate the four ways for getting attention listed on the transparency. Then call students up front, assign one of the ways on the transparency and have them practice the techniques.

5. Divide the class into four groups and have each group play a card game or Dominoes. (Let each group decide which game to play.)

   Go around the room selecting students from different groups. Tell them which way to get attention (from the transparency) and which person/group to go to. Give feedback and continue with other students.

Maintaining Conversations

1. Write on the board:

Ways to maintain conversations:

1) controlling the pace of conversation
   a) listener's behaviors
   b) signer's behaviors

2) resuming the conversation
   a) signer resumes topic after interruption and/or digression
   b) signer asks listener where s/he left off

Create situations as described below to introduce the different ways listed on the board.

Controlling the pace of conversation

2. Show the *bottom* half (Controlling the Pace of Conversation) of the "Conversation Strategies" transparency (see Materials Appendix, p. 202). Demonstrate what both the listener and the signer do to control the pace of conversation.

First tell the class to watch you as you listen to someone narrating. Then call on someone to tell you some news or a story. While you listen, do the following:

- look for something from your purse, daypack, or briefcase; and/or
- move something, i.e., table, desk, objects on table; and/or
- go get something from a cabinet, shelf or desk

Be sure to maintain eye contact with the signer while doing these things.

Switch roles and tell the other person to get something from his/her daypack, purse, etc., and demonstrate the signer's behaviors listed on the transparency.

3. After reviewing the techniques with the class, call three students up to role play listeners. Tell one to look for something, another to move something, and the third to go get something while listening. You narrate something, then give them feed-back on their behaviors as listeners.

Then call four students up front. Tell one of them to narrate something and assign the others tasks to do while listening. Give feedback on both signer's and listeners' behaviors.

4. Divide the class into groups of four or five students each. Assign each person in the group a different function (i.e., narrate; or look for something, move something, get something while listening). Remind the person who narrates to make sure all listeners are paying attention, and to slow down or repeat if one of them is looking for something.

Resuming the conversation

5. Write on the board:

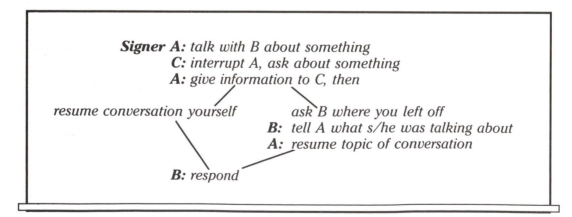

Signer A: *talk with B about something*
C: *interrupt A, ask about something*
A: *give information to C, then*

resume conversation yourself   *ask B where you left off*
         B: *tell A what s/he was talking about*
         A: *resume topic of conversation*

B: *respond*

6. Call two students up to role play Signers B and C, while you role play Signer A. After Signer C interrupts you the first time, demonstrate phrases for resuming the conversation yourself:

```
T: ANYWAY, THAT-ONE...
                        whq
   JUST-NOW ME SAY #WHAT, OH-I-SEE...

   ANYWAY, ME [OFF-POINT] BACK-TO-POINT [THAT-ONE]*...
```

After each phrase, continue the original conversation.

Then repeat the dialogue, but this time after C's interruption, ask Signer B where you left off:

```
                            whq
T: JUST-NOW ME SAY #WHAT.
```

Signer B should remind you what you were talking about.

7. Divide the class into groups of three. Tell students to follow the dialogue format, engaging in conversation about some topic, then practice all three phrases used to resume the topic of conversation. Afterwards, have them switch roles so that all students practice being Signer A.

Confirming Questions

1. Write on the board:

> **Signer A:** *ask for confirmation of a statement*
> **B:** *confirm, clarify or correct*
> **A:** *respond*

Explain that you will sign three different dialogues. Tell students to pay attention to the first sentence in all three dialogues.

2. Role play both Signers A and B in the following dialogues. Use these phrases to ask for confirmation:

```
        q                  q                  q
REAL/TRUE            RIGHT              QMwg
```

---

*NOTE: This phrase is used after a long digression to another topic, or a long discussion of one detail.

```
                                           _____q
A: POSS DAUGHTER DEAF, RIGHT.
B: YES, 1 DAUGHTER DEAF, OTHER SON HARD-OF-HEARING.
A: OH-I-SEE.
```

```
    _____t____  _____q
A: NAME fs-KATZ ITSELF JEWISH NAME, QMwg.
B: SEEM++, SHOULD #BE.
    ___nod___
A: "well".
```

```
                                        _____q
A: ME HEAR fs-LISA MOVE-AWAY AUSTRALIA, REAL/TRUE.
    _____neg_____
B: #NO, NOT MOVE-AWAY. IX PLAN STAY"there" 3-4 MONTH, TRAVEL,
   WORK. #BACK"here" FUTURE FALL.
    _____q_      _____q
A: REAL/TRUE... IX HAVE FRIEND IX-loc"Australia".
```

Ask students to repeat the questions. Explain that all three phrases are possible for confirming, but that each has its own meaning, i.e.:

```
    ___q
```
RIGHT: you are quite positive your information is correct, but you want to confirm it

```
        ___q
```
REAL/TRUE: you heard a rumor and want to check it out with someone who
   may know

```
    ___q
```
QMwg: a) you are unsure about doing something and want to ask another
         person's opinion
      b) you present a hypothetical situation and ask if it is true, or if it could
         happen that way
      c) you are curious about some information and want to know if others agree

3. Show the "Is That So?" transparencies (see Materials Appendix, pp. 203–204). Have students practice appropriate question forms and confirming phrases. Then call on pairs of students to go through the dialogue format for each statement.

Students should come up with ASL question forms like the following:

                                                                 q
Statement A: FIRST-*thumb* DAY WINTER, fs-DEC 21, RIGHT.

                                                 t   q
Statement B: PERSON ESTABLISH GALLAUDET COLLEGE, SELF HEARING, RIGHT.

                                          t   q
Statement C: FIRST-*thumb* PERSON TOUCH MOON, NAME fs-ARMSTRONG, RIGHT.

                                 q
Statement D: RIGHT, ELEPHANT CONCEIVE, PREGNANT 2+YEAR, GIVE-BIRTH-

                                 q
TO, RIGHT.

---

                                                      q
Statement E: HEAR fs-JFK !MANY! GIRL+FRIEND, REAL/TRUE.

Statement F: SOMEONE TELL-TO-*me* FUTURE WEDNESDAY SIGN LANGUAGE

                              q
CLASS CANCEL, REAL/TRUE.

                                            q
Statement G: ME HEAR WATER HERE NOT+GOOD, DIRTY, REAL/TRUE.

                                          q
Statement H: ME HEAR fs-ELVIS HAVE 2 DAUGHTER, REAL/TRUE.

---

                            t   q
Statement I: IX-loc MEXICO, DRINK WATER #OK, QMwg.

                                      q
Statement J: GO-TO WORKSHOP !IMPORTANT! QMwg.

Statement K: QMwg NOTHING-TO-IT [ME] MEET BOSS COMPLAIN,

                             q
NOTHING-TO-IT QMwg.

---

                                                                cond
Statement L: SUPPOSE ME BUY AIRPLANE TICKET 3-WEEKS-FUTURE,

                              q
INCREASE COST QMwg.

                                                         cond
Statement M: SUPPOSE JAPAN MACHINE/ENGINE (2h)PUT-IN AMERICA CAR,

                             q
WILL DESTROY QMwg.

Statement N: SUPPOSE NEEDLE [(wh)LCL:1*"end above fire"*/ECL:5wg*"flame under*

                cond   q
needle"] [IX*"needle"*] WILL !CLEAN! QMwg.

Statement O: fs-WELLS-FARGO OPEN EVERY-SATURDAY QMwg.
$\overline{\hspace{5cm}}^{q}$

Statement P: fs-LELYVELD ITSELF NORWAY NAME QMwg.
$\overline{\hspace{2cm}}^{t}$ $\overline{\hspace{3cm}}^{q}$

Statement Q: PERFORMANCE, HAVE INTERPRET[+ER] QMwg.
$\overline{\hspace{2cm}}^{t}$ $\overline{\hspace{3.5cm}}^{q}$

Statement R: MAN IX, GENERATION DEAF, QMwg.
$\overline{\hspace{1.5cm}}^{t}$ $\overline{\hspace{3cm}}^{q}$

Asking for Help with the Spelling of Names

1. Write on the board:

> **Situation:** *Signer A wants to talk about someone or something, but can only think of the first few letters of the name.*
>
> **Signer A:** *describe someone/something, ask for help with spelling the name*
>   **B:** *spell name*
>   **A:** *respond*

Role play Signer A. Describe a person or an object and begin to spell the name, then act like you're unsure of how to spell it. Tell students to be Signer B and try to complete the spelling of the name. Encourage them to ask for more information to help pinpoint the name.

For example, describe a student in class named Ramona, then say:

> $\overline{\hspace{5cm}}^{t}$ $\overline{\hspace{4cm}}^{unsure}$
> **T:** KNOW+ (describe person, (ME) THINK NAME fs-RA+"imaginary line"...

Demonstrate Signer A's responses to B's suggestions:

respond

> YES !THAT-ONE! . . . .(positively right)
> SEEM++ THAT-ONE . . . .(could be correct)
> $\overline{\hspace{4cm}}^{neg}$
> "wave-no" NOT+THAT-ONE . . . .(positively wrong)

2. Continue role playing Signer A in other dialogues in which you:
   • describe a person in class, or a well-known person on campus
   • describe a famous person, i.e., actor/actress, current or past President of U.S., a sports figure
   • describe a brand-name product

3. Cut out pictures of comic-strip characters and brand-name products and paste them onto index cards. (Or have students find pictures and bring them to class.) Distribute the cards to students.

Tell students to follow the dialogue format, describing the characters or objects on their cards and spelling out only the first few letters of the name, then following with a dash.

The rest of the class should try to guess the name of the object or character.

━━■BREAKAWAY

NUMBERS

Go Fish
(see Appendix, p. 198)

INTERACTION

After the Vacation

Purpose: To give students practice in keeping each other informed about relevant things.

1. Write the following situation on the board:

> *Mary has just returned from her vacation. She and her housesitter, Darah, meet again to share what happened during her absence.*

Divide the class into four groups, assigning the role of either Mary or Darah to each group.

2. Tell each group to come up with five different things that happened during Mary's absence. The "Darah" group should create five incidents around the house, i.e., things that happened with the lamp, the dog, neighbors, mail. The "Mary" group should create five incidents that occurred on her trip. They may choose any location for the trip.

Before they break into groups, instruct all students to change their appearance in a distracting way, i.e., turn their collar up (or down), put lipstick or chalk marks on their faces, put a scrap of paper or a leaf in their hair.

Then, during the group discussion, each student should practice telling another group member that something is distracting them.

191

3. After the group discussion, pair off students (with one from a "Mary" group and one from a "Darah" group in each pair). Have students use the ideas created by their group to exchange stories about what happened.

Making Connections

Purpose: To continue developing skills for keeping each other informed by sharing information about ourselves and others.

1. Show the "Making Connections" transparency (see Materials Appendix, p. 205). Select one student to be the interviewer and the other to be the good friend. You role play the focus person in Situations 1 and 2. Have the two students ask you questions about the topics on the transparency. Demonstrate how to share general information with the interviewer and give detailed information to the good friend. For example:

<u>With Interviewer</u>   <u>With Good Friend</u>

family

- tell that you have three brothers and sisters

- add that one of your siblings is adopted, or gay, or that there was one more sibling who died young, etc.

educational background

- tell that you worked at a community college

- add that you hated that job, or were fired, or you produced a videotape there, etc.

occupation

- tell that you went to college and majored in English

- add that you wanted to major in Biology, but you hated the teachers there, or that you were class president during your sophomore year

2. Now have the interviewer and good friend role play Situation 3. They should share information they learned from talking with you, so they both are equally informed.

Tell the good friend to use this phrase with appropriate conversation regulators for interrupting:

                              q
_____
KNOW-THAT. . .

At appropriate times during their conversation, introduce the following phrases for the interviewer:

          q   neg
_____   _____
REAL/TRUE. ME NOT-KNOW.

neg

IX NOT TELL-TO-*me*.

OH-I-SEE. INTERESTING.
whq

WHO TELL-TO-*you* WHO.

3. Divide the class into groups of three students. Assign one of the three roles (interviewer, focus person and good friend) to each student in the group. Then follow this procedure:

   Situation 1: Begin by telling all Signers C (good friends) to leave the room, leaving Signers A and B to have their dialogue in privacy.

   Situation 2: When the interview is done, tell all Signers A to leave the room to rehearse the information learned in the interview. Call Signers C into the room. Tell Signers B and C to proceed with Situation 2 on the transparency.

   Situation 3: Afterwards, tell Signers B (focus persons) to sit in a corner of the room and observe. Call in Signers A (interviewers) to have a dialogue with Signers C, sharing information they have about the focus persons.

   Remind students to use phrases for returning to a previous topic of conversation, and phrases for responding to information.

4. Repeat this activity until each student has had a chance to become the focus person.

EXTENDED COMPREHENSION

Videotaped Narratives

1. Show the videotaped narrative **"Lost Keys"** in which Lee Ann Poynor explains how she found a set of car keys that had been missing for a few weeks.

2. Ask students questions about the narrative:

Questions	Answers
a) Who borrowed the keys?	(Lee Ann's daughter)
b) Where did Lee Ann think her daughter left the keys?	(on the table)
c) Where did she look for the keys?	(on the table, around the kitchen sink, and under the pile of letters)
d) Where did the granddaughter say the keys were?	(in the bedroom closet)

e) What did Lee Ann dream about one night several weeks later?

(finding the keys)

f) Who came the next morning and what did she want?

(Lee Ann's sister came to borrow some folding chairs)

g) Where did Lee Ann find the missing keys?

(right there in the bedroom closet where the folding chairs were stored)

h) What did Lee Ann say about her granddaughter?

(that she wasn't making up the story about the keys)

3. Point out the narrative techniques Lee Ann used:

Use of space: She used the signing space in front of her to locate where things are, i.e.: the kitchen table in front of her, the kitchen sink to her left, the pile of letters to her right, and then the bedroom to her right.

Use of pronouns: She used IX and SCL:1 in specific locations around her signing space to refer to different people, i.e.: the daughter coming in from the right, the granddaughter coming in from the right, her sister coming in from the left.

Notice how she used IX *"right"* in the last sentence to refer to her granddaughter, after locating her in that area earlier in the narrative.

Role shifting: She used role shifting to indicate who is speaking:

                                                             whq

< *rs:Lee Ann* ME TAP-SHOULDER DAUGHTER, WHERE MY KEY >.

< *rs:daughter* SAY IX *"table in front"* TABLE IX >.

fs-GRAND+DAUGHTER SCL:1*"came up to me"* TAP-*me-on-thigh* < *rs:grand-daughter* KEY IX *"there"* KEY >.

< *rs:Lee Ann* ME FOLLOW-*her* BED+ROOM...(bending over) THANK-YOU FOR HELP+. ME WANT CAR KEY. THANK-YOU >.

TOMORROW MORNING ME < *rs:Lee Ann* TAP-SHOULDER DAUGHTER, ME DREAM MY KEY ICL*"hold keys up"*... >

MY SISTER M-*on-chest* SCL:1*"came up to me"*, < *rs:Lee Ann* HELLO, (YOU) WANT LEND-TO-*you* FOLDING CHAIR. FINE+ >.

Time frame: She established a time frame in her narrative by using time phrases and long pauses:

ONE TIME...
... DO-ERRANDS...
FOR SEVERAL WEEK, THAT NIGHT...
TOMORROW MORNING...
... (pause, arms folded) MY SISTER...

4. Sign parts of the narrative again and have students repeat after you. Be sure students use appropriate narrative techniques.

   Then divide the class into several small groups. Have students in each group repeat the narrative again. The other students in the group should give listener feedback while watching the narrative.

5. Preview the videotaped narrative **"My Family Roots"** by Ken Pedersen for vocabulary and phrases used. (You may want to show it at a later date if the narrative seems too difficult for your students to follow.)

   In the narrative, Ken talks about his family history: his sister's trip to Europe to visit their ancestors' birthplaces and burial sites, and the history of deafness in his family.

6. Show the "My Family Roots" transparency (see Materials Appendix, p. 206).

7. Point to each part of the outline on the transparency and tell the same story to the class that Ken told on videotape. That way you can introduce vocabulary before students see it on tape:

NORWAY	DROP-JAW
FINLAND	ESCAPE
SWEDEN	PRECEDING-GENERATIONS
DENMARK	(2h)alt.LOOK-AT
fs-SCANDINAVIAN	SATISFIED
ECL"snap pictures"	DCL"roots"
BORN+PLACE (birth place)	INVESTIGATE
fs-MILANO	FIND
MILANO	

   Then show the videotape, and follow up with questions about the narrative.

8. Discuss how Ken identified the two towns his sister visited. Rather than spell out the names of the towns, he located them by their proximity to a large city (Milano), and to the Arctic Circle (where the sun doesn't set during the summer).

   Also, show how Ken described the sun circling the earth. This is what the eye sees, in spite of the fact that it is actually the earth circling the sun.

9. Ask students questions about their family roots:

   • Have you ever investigated your family roots?
   • Have any members of your family escaped from their country of origin?
   • How is your surname different from what it was originally?
   • Go back several generations — any deaf people? any with red hair?
     any gap-toothed? etc.

10. Show the "Map of Canada" transparency (see Materials Appendix, p. 207). Identify places and towns on the map by first pointing to a town (i.e., Saskatoon) and showing where it is located in relation to the nearest large city, i.e.:

> ```
>                                q/t
> ```
> **T:** ME LIVE NEAR KNOW fs-CALGARY [(wh)IX-loc*"Calgary"/* IX-loc*"east of Calgary"*].

Point to another town on the map, i.e., Victoria, and sign:

> ```
>                                           t/q
> ```
> **T:** MY GRANDMOTHER BORN IX-loc, KNOW VANCOUVER, [(wh)IX-loc*"Vancouver"/*IX-loc*"southwest of Vancouver"*].

Now point to other towns on the map, i.e., Banff, Kingston, Sault Ste. Marie, and ask where they are located. Be sure students use reference points correctly.

Have students pretend they are telling people from out of state where they live. They should establish the location of their town in relation to the nearest large city in the state.

The Lost Ring

1. Hand out copies of "The Lost Ring" activity sheet (see Materials Appendix, p. 208). Then tell a story about looking for a lost ring (see outline on next page). Students are to number their worksheet according to the locations in your story where you looked for the ring.

2. In your story, use as many DCLs, ICLs, and LCLs as possible to show how to visualize the place, the action taken, and the relationship of one location to another. Use this sequence when telling about movement from one location to another:

> ```
>                 t
> ```
> **T:** (identify location), (tell activity using DCL, ICL, LCL).

Also use the sign NONE when at each location you do not find the ring.

3. Outline of the story:

Introduction

Last Saturday you went to the park and spent a lovely day there. When you arrived home you discovered your ring was missing.

Body

The next day you went back to the park to look for your ring.

1) you looked inside the overturned boat
2) you looked in the squirrel's hole and ran your hand through the nuts
3) you crossed the bridge over to the parking lot, looked in between and underneath the cars
4) you walked under the waterfall, up the hill, and looked around the base of the tree
5) you went back down the hill, over to the concession stand, looked inside the garbage can
6) you went over to the play area, climbed the ladder, looked in the play house, then you looked over by the swing, then you looked over by the see-saw; you got down on your hands and knees and ran your hands through the sand
7) you went over to the picnic tables, looked under and around both tables, you lifted the barbecue cover and looked inside
8) you looked under the bushes
9) you looked up on top of the bush, lifted the bird off its nest, felt in the nest, then set the bird back down
10) exhausted, you lay down to take a nap and dreamt you found the ring. Waking up, you sat up and saw the duck island right in front of you. You waded in the water. There in the water next to the island you saw a shiny object. You reached in the water and pulled out your ring. You were so relieved!

---

4. Have students repeat the story. Begin by signing the introduction yourself, then:

- have the first student sign the first place you looked
- have the second student repeat the first place, then add the second place
- have the third student repeat the first two places, then add the third place, etc.

Continue until students have repeated the entire story. Make sure students use the sequence of first identifying the location, then telling the activity. Also monitor for consistency in referring to established locations, and their use of DCLs, ICLs, and LCLs.

Variation: Each student can make up his/her own story and tell it to a partner, who in turn labels the map according to the new version.

STUDENT VIDEOTEXT AND WORKBOOK

1. Make sure students complete the video-interactive and other activities for this unit, either in class or for homework. Also assign the Culture/Language Notes for this unit.

End of Cumulative Review: Units 13 – 17

APPENDIX

NUMBERS

Go Fish

1. Make a deck of cards for each group of five to seven students in your class (i.e., for a class of 18, make three sets).

   Each deck of cards should include two cards of each of the numbers below (a total of 60 cards):

$8.00	$1.50	4276 Fern	Oct. 6, 1942	111
8:00	1:50	4287 Fern	Oct. 9, 1942	101
12 cents	6:45	Jan. 5, 1939	5269 48th Ave.	1860's
12 years old	$6.45	June 5, 1939	5269 47th Ave.	1960's
5th	4:00	Sept. 15, 1975	Feb. 1789	11:15
$5.00	4	Sept. 15, 1985	Feb. 1798	1:15

2. Divide the class into groups of five to seven players. Give each group a deck of cards. They should deal out five to six cards to each player and put the remaining cards face down in the middle.

3. Each player must try to find the match for every card in his/her hand. At each turn, a player asks another player if s/he has a _____ (signing exactly what is on a card). Make sure students use the correct number form.

   If the other player doesn't have the match, s/he tells the first player to "go fish" and the first player has to pick from the pile. If the first player guessed right and gets the matching card (or if s/he picks the matching card from the pile), s/he gets another turn.

4. The first player to get a match for every card in his/her hand wins the game.

1) Why did it take Cinnie so long to bring the food?

2) What do the women think about the weather?

3) How did the Deaf man in the line know Cinnie is Deaf?

4) How did Cinnie feel when she found out the man is Deaf?
Why?

5) What is the Deaf man's name? How do he and Mary know each other?

6) What is Nick's wife's job?

7) How many children do they have? Which one(s) are Deaf?

8) Who do the children resemble?

9) What role does Nick have in the Deaf community?

You begin the activity. Pick up a piece of paper and throw it into the wastebasket.

When you see someone throwing a piece of paper into the wastebasket, get everyone's attention, then tell your classmates that your house is shaped like a geodesic dome, is made of glass, and has a white picket fence.

After someone has given a description of his/her house, get everyone's attention and instruct them to make one full turn, then to shake hands with the people standing next to them.

After people have shaken hands, get everyone's attention and tell them that you (or your wife) just gave birth to twins.

After someone has announced the birth of twins, get everyone's attention, then take out your keys and explain what each key is for.

After someone talks about his/her keys, get everyone's attention and announce that your cat had a litter of six kittens. Then ask if anyone wants to have a kitten.

After someone asks if anyone wants a kitten, walk around the room, pause, then get everyone's attention. Ask if anyone has seen your mouse.

When someone asks about a mouse, get everyone's attention and tell them you saw a mouse earlier, picked it up and put it in the teacher's desk.

When someone tells what was put in the teacher's desk, get everyone's attention and tell them that you taped a five-dollar bill under the seat of one of the chairs in the room. Instruct the class to look for it.

When people begin to look under the chairs, get everyone's attention and tell them the person who told them to look for something under a chair is a liar.

After someone says that another person is a liar, get everyone's attention and ask if anyone has nail clippers with them.

After someone asks for nail clippers, get everyone's attention and announce that a taxi is here. Ask who called for a taxi.

After someone announces that a taxi is here, get everyone's attention, hold up a pencil and ask who it belongs to.

After someone asks who a pencil belongs to, get everyone's attention and play a joke: point to a specific location (for example, the ceiling) and ask everyone if they see a nail there. After everyone has failed to find the nail, point out that it is the nail on your finger you were referring to.

After someone plays a joke about a nail, get everyone's attention and lavish praise on your Sign Language teacher. Get everyone to agree.

After someone lavishes praise on the teacher, get everyone's attention and tell them all to line up according to age.

After people line up according to age, get everyone's attention and suggest that the next class session be held at the park.

After someone suggests that class be held at the park, get everyone's attention and tell them to find someone else in class who has the same astrological sign.

After everyone has found another person with the same astrological sign, get everyone's attention and tell them to sit down and give their attention to the teacher.

GETTING ATTENTION

1. Approach the group and get one person's attention, then ask a question as privately as possible.

2. Get the attention of one person in the group without approaching the group, then ask a question.

3. Get someone in the group to direct the attention of a particular person to you, then ask a question.

4. Approach the group and get everyone's attention, then ask a question.

CONTROLLING THE PACE OF CONVERSATION

Listener's Behaviors

• make quick glances away at appropriate times
• nod to indicate that the signer can go ahead with the story

Signer's Behaviors

• hold signs or slow down signs
• repeat signs
• adjust position or move around

Check if the **information** below is correct:

Statement A: The first day of winter is December 21.

Statement B: The founder of Gallaudet University
was hearing.

Statement C: Armstrong was the first person to walk
on the moon.

Statement D: An elephant's pregnancy lasts two years.

Check if the **rumors** below are true:

Statement E: John F. Kennedy had many girlfriends.

Statement F: The next Sign Language class session
will be cancelled.

Statement G: The tap water in your area is polluted.

Statement H: Elvis Presley had two daughters.

Check others' **opinions** about the statements below:

Statement I: It's all right to drink tap water
in Mexico.

Statement J: It's worthwhile to attend the workshop.

Statement K: It's all right to complain to your boss.

Check if the **hypothetical situations** below could be true:

Statement L: If you wait a few weeks to buy your airline ticket, the fare will go up.

Statement M: If you install a Japanese-made engine in an American car, you'll damage the car.

Statement N: Putting a needle over a flame will sterilize the needle.

You're curious about the following information. Check if others **agree.**

Statement O: A certain bank will be open on Saturday.

Statement P: The name Lelyveld is Norweigan.

Statement Q: The play has an interpreter for Deaf people.

Statement R: Deafness runs in a certain person's family.

Players: interviewer, focus person and good friend

Situation 1: An interviewer asks the focus person general questions about his/her life.

> Topics: family
> educational background
> occupation

Situation 2: The focus person talks with a good friend to share more detailed or personal information about the topics above.

Situation 3: The interviewer talks with the good friend. They both share information about the focus person.

Focus Person
(A)
will tell

Interviewer (B)	Good Friend (C)
the following general information:	the following detailed information:
family	family
how many brothers and sisters or children	relationships with others
— their names	occupations
— their ages	likes and dislikes
marriages	family secrets
	talents and accomplishments
	nationality
	divorces/remarriages
educational background	educational background
degrees, if any	accomplishments or achievements
names of schools/colleges	failures
major	likes and dislikes
	extracurricular activities
	positions held
occupation	occupation
position title	opinions
place of work	specific responsibilities
	accomplishments
	office gossip

Introduction

Ken Pedersen's immediate family members are all Deaf.

- His mother's side is Italian (Ponsetti).
- His father's side is Scandinavian (Tinsett).

Body

- When Ken was a child, his father died. His maternal grandfather raised Ken's family.
- His grandfather died a few years ago. Ken's sister started thinking about family roots and decided to fly to Europe the previous summer.
- She went to her grandfather's birthplace in a town near Milano. She visited the graveyard of the Ponsetti family, and also the house where her grandfather used to live. (He left Italy at the age of 15.)
- She flew to a small town in the north of Finland (near the Arctic Circle) and saw the graveyard of the Tinsett family.
- On her return to the States, she shared the photographs from her trip with her family.

Closing

Ken's sister's curiosity was still not satisfied. She wanted to know if there had been any ancestors who were Deaf. She traced the family roots and found that they had many Deaf ancestors.

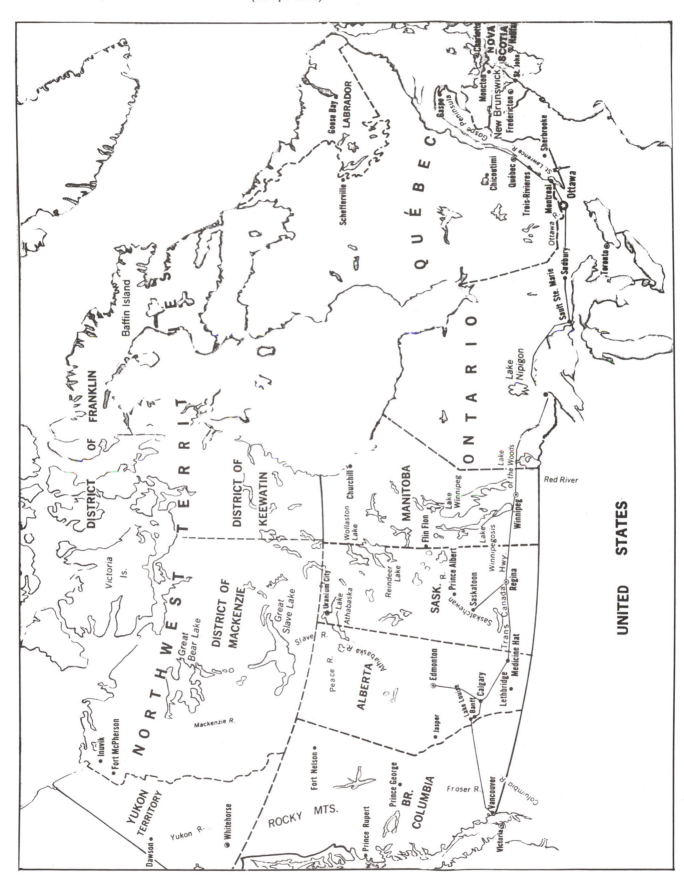

"THE LOST RING"
(for p. 196)
Activity Sheet